D0006994

8/2023
STRAND PRICE
$5 00

# DID
# THAT
## JUST HAPPEN?!

# DID
# THAT
## JUST HAPPEN?!

*Beyond "Diversity"—Creating*
*Sustainable and Inclusive Organizations*

. . . . . . .

## DR. STEPHANIE PINDER-AMAKER
## AND DR. LAUREN WADSWORTH

BEACON PRESS
Boston

BEACON PRESS
Boston, Massachusetts
www.beacon.org

Beacon Press books
are published under the auspices of
the Unitarian Universalist Association of Congregations.

© 2021 by Stephanie Pinder-Amaker and Lauren Wadsworth

All rights reserved
Printed in the United States of America

24 23 22 21    8 7 6 5 4 3 2 1

This book is printed on acid-free paper that meets the uncoated paper
ANSI/NISO specifications for permanence as revised in 1992.

Text design and composition by Kim Arney

*Library of Congress Cataloging-in-Publication Data*

Names: Pinder-Amaker, Stephanie, author. | Wadsworth, Lauren, author.
Title: Did that just happen?! : beyond "diversity"—creating sustainable
and inclusive organizations / Stephanie Pinder-Amaker, PhD,
and Lauren Wadsworth, PhD.
Description: Boston : Beacon Press, 2021. | Includes bibliographical
references and index.
Identifiers: LCCN 2021003308 (print) | LCCN 2021003309 (ebook) |
ISBN 9780807035887 (hardcover ; alk. paper) | ISBN 9780807035894 (ebook)
Subjects: LCSH: Diversity in the workplace. | Multiculturalism. | Racism. |
Intercultural communication. | Discrimination in employment.
Classification: LCC HF5549.5.M5 P56 2021 (print) |
LCC HF5549.5.M5 (ebook) | DDC 658.3008—dc23
LC record available at https://lccn.loc.gov/2021003308
LC ebook record available at https://lccn.loc.gov/2021003309

*We dedicate this book to each other for having the patience and trust required to teach and learn together, and to the great authors who paved the way for us by writing about what it's like to be Black, Indigenous, a Person of Color, queer, disabled, or to hold any rising identity . . . so that we could quote and reference you. Thank you for saving us and countless others the emotional labor of having to describe these experiences.*

# CONTENTS

# AUTHORS' NOTE

THIS BOOK IS FOR ORGANIZATIONS—COMPANIES, SCHOOLS, and nonprofits—and the people working within those settings who are aiming to create cultures that are sustainably diverse and inclusive. We provide advice for both organizational leadership and individuals at all levels. We believe that truly inclusive organizations require consistent, long-term investment by leadership (financially, emotionally, and educationally). We also believe that diversity, equity, and inclusion (DEI) efforts, even when laid out well by leadership, will not succeed if the individuals within the organization are not adept at working, speaking, and healing across different identities (for instance, Latinx and white, gay and straight).

We open our book by addressing a few limitations. Throughout we speak largely from our personal experiences and identities. Both authors identify as cisgender women who were born in the United States and have been US citizens their entire lives. Neither of us has Indigenous heritage or a disability. We have attempted to include vignettes and examples that represent a multitude of sociocultural identities; however, we realize that some readers may not see themselves explicitly represented in these pages. We hope that the recommendations will be considered both in the context of the identities mentioned in the examples (such as race), and also generalized to other identities by the readers.

While the vignettes are largely based in the United States and, thus, our sociocultural politics, the skills we impart are applicable cross-culturally, with attention to the fact that it is more or less acceptable to speak out in different regions of the world, based on identity (for example, as a woman, as someone from a lower socioeconomic status, or a nondominant religion). The vignettes are based on true stories as shared with and experienced by us. Our aim in sharing these narratives is not to embarrass but to educate. Therefore, in many instances, we have changed identifying characteristics, including name, location, and type of organization or industry.

We will share ideas that some disagree with and leave out things unintentionally that people will be upset we missed. As this work evolves, some of our suggestions will become outdated. As we write, language is continuously shifting within the DEI and anti-racism literatures. This book is meant to be easily digestible, with tangible takeaway skills throughout each chapter. One cost of this approach is that we do not heavily review the many incredible scholars who have come before us in this field. For developing deeper knowledge on the origin of these concepts, we recommend readings in realms such as racism, power and privilege, anti-racism, and white privilege.

A few notes on the terms that we use throughout this book. When we say "organization," we are referring to any structured group of people. Thus, this book is meant to apply to schools, research and healthcare institutions, businesses of all sizes, and nonprofit organizations. Oftentimes the words "diversity" and "inclusion" are used interchangeably. We use the term "sociocultural identities" to describe the many identities we all hold. As psychologists, we often use our adapted ADDRESSING framework, which is an acronym that reminds us of the sociocultural identities that have historically been dominant or targeted (age, disability, diagnosis [mental health], religion, race, ethnicity, socioeconomic status, sexual orientation, Indigenous heritage, nation of origin/citizenship status, and gender identity and gender expression).[1] When we say "diverse," we are referring to a group of people that includes representation across many sociocultural identities (for example, a group that includes people of many different races or gender identities). When we say "inclusive," we mean that the organization/group is aware of the history of dominant and targeted identities and is aiming to work against those dynamics. Inclusive organizations are reflective, considerate of positionality, and aim to engage in a process of continued learning on the topic of sociocultural identities—like reading this book.

CHAPTER 1

# INCLUSIVE TEAMS
# ARE BETTER TEAMS

W E ARE AT AN INFLECTION POINT. THE TIMELINE OF THE
past few years, a steady drumbeat of a world unjust, birthed
this book. We were able to write it because we have developed a
deep, trusting relationship. That relationship has elevated our work
to greater levels. We have seen, firsthand, the benefit of having a "diverse" team. We know that relationships across difference can transform not only individuals, but also the greater system around them.
We believe that by developing and sustaining relationships across
difference like we have, we can build empathy in spaces where stereotypes and bias once stood.

We developed our relationship using a number of skills that we
were taught or that we developed together. We believe those skills
can easily translate to all workplaces, educational settings, and organizations. Thus we share them with you, using real-life, de-identified,
stories. We identify where things went wrong and provide guidance
on what to do next. We believe that by engaging these skills you can
enhance your relationships, create sustainably diverse teams, and reduce bias in the workplace and the world.

■ ■ ■ ■ ■ ■ ■

•  Jaymie's Story  •

*The day was finally here. After years of college courses, networking, apprenticeships, and dreaming, Jaymie, a Latinx queer woman, studied her reflection in the full-length mirror. As she straightened her blouse and donned her suit jacket, she wondered if her attire was "feminine" enough to meet people's expectations and "masculine" enough to be taken seriously. Only one interview away from landing her dream internship at a major advertising agency, she arrived early and confidently navigated the bank of slick glass elevators to the fourteenth floor. As she strode into the firm's lobby, she caught another quick glimpse of herself, adjusted her hair, and thought,* Yikes. Am I wearing too much eyeshadow?

*Upon entering the office suite, she was ushered to a conference room where she joined the other interviewees. They nodded and smiled while sizing one another up, pretending not to be competitors. The directors, two older white men, entered the room. They spoke passionately about the history of the agency and shared their vision for the future of the company. As the session came to a close, the senior director slowly scanned the room and said, "We have been told by interns in the past that they were disappointed by the lack of diversity in our workforce. We want you to hear it directly from us: we are working to change that."* Promising. *Jaymie felt the eyes dart to and away from her, so fast it was hard to discern if it had really happened.*

*One month later, Jaymie got the long-anticipated call: "You're in!" Still, it took days for it to sink in. Landing this coveted internship would all but guarantee a prosperous career as a creative in the advertising world. One hundred percent of the agency's interns would be offered permanent jobs there or in other leading agencies. Despite Jaymie's excitement, day one of the internship began with a familiar angst as she pondered the possible permutations and implications of her many outfit choices.* If I wear a dress with heels, will they think I'm trying to look sexy to get ahead at work? Am I overcompensating for being queer, dressing in this predictably feminine way? *Pushing these thoughts aside, Jaymie made her selections, dressed, and arrived early to begin life at the agency.*

*Jaymie took her place among the other "chosen ones" gathered around the conference table. She immediately began to calculate the identities rep-*

resented by the internship class. Knowing that the advertising world is historically very homogenous, she was excited not to be the only woman or person of color in the room. One Asian American. Check. Fifty percent women. Check. During the small talk, the only Black intern, Dan, came out to her, sharing that he and his male partner had just returned from a trip to Canada. Double check. Clearly, the directors had honored their commitment to creating a more diverse workforce. Bravo! Dan and Jaymie joked quietly about being part of the "diversity initiative on steroids."

Soon, however, the familiar pains of a diverse workforce being created in a space where there had previously been only a trace of one began to emerge. Jaymie's Asian American colleague was approached about a new account: "We need an ad geared toward low-income people. We want you to come up with some ethnic ideas." Did that just happen?! Later the team was critiquing Dan's draft of an advertisement for a popular clothing company, to be aired during Pride Month. "These men are too tough-looking to be gay," said one of the creatives, who refused to back down. Men regularly dominated the meetings, talking over women unapologetically. And in December, with total disregard for their Jewish and Muslim colleagues, company leadership arranged for Christmas wreaths to adorn all the halls and had each employee get their photo taken with Santa at a company Christmas party. The intern director made transphobic jokes, calling the first mainstream gender-neutral actor on a new hit show "it." Dan, meanwhile, was frequently confused for environmental services staff. Jaymie and her peers grew increasingly frustrated and disillusioned. With each incident the interns thought, All right, this is the moment. Someone in leadership is definitely going to say something this time. Crickets. Nothing.

After four months they decided to share their collective concerns and experiences as a cohort. They were met with mixed messages from the directors. One team leader expressed gratitude that the interns had shared their thoughts but was quick to add, "You have to realize how far we've come. We've already changed a lot." Another leader chimed in: "I think your generation is just too sensitive and quick to assign blame. Your class should be grateful that we're giving you this opportunity." "Further," they were chastised, "if you have a problem, just say it! Don't wait so long to *speak up." Following the meeting, Jaymie received one-on-one feedback from a supervisor, who told her she was like "a bull in a china shop" and that she needed to be less forthcoming with her thoughts, out of respect for those who had more expertise.*

*The year progressed and the interns stayed quiet, swallowing the hurt, anxiety, and anger that frequently climbed up their throats. Ultimately, though, Jaymie, along with two-thirds of the class, received lucrative offers to sign on permanently with the agency. Almost everyone, however, elected to go with competing agencies and Dan left advertising altogether. Although the company was well intentioned, it alienated the very talent pool it was trying to attract. The organization's leaders and managers did not understand that simply bringing in people with a diverse range of identities was not enough.*

### WHY THIS IS PROBLEMATIC: THE TWO-PART PROBLEM

We know diverse teams are better teams. The data support this and anecdotally people report it. Workforces that contain a wide range of sociocultural identities show better performance and have greater innovation.[1] Increasingly, leaders are touting their commitment to forming such diverse teams. "Sociocultural identities" refers to the multitude of identities we hold that have historically held privilege or been marginalized, such as race, religion, age, ethnicity, sexual orientation, gender, gender expression, nationality, disability/ability status, and socioeconomic status. Companies are stating in their job postings that they value diverse teams, offering candidates the option to self-identify when applying, and centralizing images of people of color on their websites while nudging each other, stating, "We need a diversity hire this time . . . okay?" Interviewers are touting their commitment to diversity and citing identity-related examples when interviewing someone they perceive as holding one or more "rising identities,"[2] a more empowering term we use instead of such standbys as "minorities" and "marginalized" when talking about groups that have been historically underrepresented.

Colleges and universities are also leaning heavily on this research, which shows that a diverse student body makes for a superior institution. Marketing teams are including diverse representation in their promotional materials and on their websites, hoping to attract students who hold a range of rising identities. In fact, most college-aged students of color we interviewed for this book laughed with a pained smile while recounting how many times they had been asked if they could be photographed for their school's brochure, contrasted with white peers who had never been asked. And these efforts are paying off. Over the past decade, diversity among US college students across sociocultural identities has increased exponentially.

Against this backdrop, it might be easy to think that we are facilitating important change. But while we may be getting better at *creating* diverse teams, we are not very good at *sustaining* them. Diverse teams come with more identity-based pain, as the generational waves, with their disparate skills and knowledge about what it means to practice inclusivity and equity, collide in the workplace. Employees who hold rising identities experience subtle and outward oppression, often committed subconsciously, from those who have historically been in power (white men), who have not had a lot of practice working with people different from themselves. Stereotypes and biases surface; people get hurt. Subsequently, folks with rising identities move on to different settings. Diversifying our workforces requires a two-part commitment: not only is it necessary to hire more employees with rising identities, but we must also transform the institutions themselves to make them inclusive and sustainable.

Building an inclusive team does not stop at checking off boxes. Merely celebrating because "My workforce is approximately 50 percent female, check; my team is 40 percent people of color, check; I have a high percentage of trans* employees, check" is not enough. ("Trans*" is an inclusive way to refer to the range of identities within the "trans/transgender" umbrella.) In fact, this is merely where the work begins. When organizations, working against generations of societal norms and expectations, create teams that are more diverse than most neighborhoods are, they are creating new and fledgling environments. In the US, these new environments are vulnerable and require attention and sustenance in order to thrive. Diverse teams are poised to unleash new ideas, cultures, inspiration, and creativity. They are also primed to promote interactions among worlds that have been separate for too long. As each member of the team seeks to find their place within the organization, planning and forethought must be given to acknowledge that people bring more than just their professional selves into the building. We must learn to welcome and value the multitude of sociocultural identities that people walk in with, those very identities and corresponding experiences that we so vigorously recruited to begin with.

Increasingly, companies and institutions are aware that recruitment and hiring efforts are insufficient for sustaining nimble and effective inclusive teams. A costly revolving-door cycle can ensue as workplace conflicts arise, people with historically rising identities burn out at faster rates, and exit interviews reveal that microaggressions were flowing more freely than bitter breakroom coffee. This repetitive chain of events, known as the leaky pipeline, can be demoralizing and frustrating but it doesn't have to be inevitable. We believe this book will help support leaders in their current diversity, equity, and inclusion efforts, or assist them as they begin to make these changes for the first time. There is a great deal that leadership and employees can do to shift the culture of the workplace, receive and support a more diverse workforce, help it to realize its potential, and yes, benefit from its creativity and strength.

### WHAT TO DO ABOUT IT: MAINTAINING DIVERSE TEAMS

The good news is, the secret to sustaining diverse teams is not being *perfect*—never making mistakes, or knowing the "complete" list of right and wrong words to utter or avoid. This work should never be about how many Black friends, employees of color, gay cousins, or multiracial grandchildren you can lay claim to. The secret to sustaining diverse teams is to make them inclusive, to shift the culture to match the shifting demographics. It is important to create and encourage workforce and academic cultures that directly acknowledge the increased complexity of diverse environments. We need to develop systems that understand that "honoring and valuing diversity" is much more than a tagline. Rather, this work requires and deserves increased institutional effort, financial investment, and expertise. We need to provide individuals with the skills to learn how to speak confidently across differences and to repair relationships when, inevitably, ruptures take place.

This book is designed to teach you the essential skills you will need to develop an ability to recognize identity-based pain and incidents, how to address them, and how to ultimately improve the culture of your workplace and the retention of your amazing, diverse team. There are, however, many more ways you can use this book. If you have been fighting this fight for a long time, pushing for diversity and inclusion, hosting these conversations, you might use this book for self-validation and further education. If you easily recognize identity-related stressors at work but lack the power to risk leading the necessary change, you might recommend this book (directly or anonymously by slipping it under an office door) to leaders in your organization and request that they use it to fuel companywide discussion and training. If you hold a leadership role and have grown weary of your institution's leaky pipeline, you might provide this book as prereading so employees can develop a shared vocabulary and skills as a starting point, then use it alongside companywide diversity and inclusion efforts and trainings. And if you are a white manager who wants to better understand these issues but you don't know where to start, look no further.

CHAPTER 2

# WHAT'S IN A NAME?

• Dr. Daisy's Story •

Adaeze Adebayo-Opeyemi arrived as a highly recruited young doctor to
a tier-one academic medical center on the West Coast. Like many young
professionals of color, she had grown accustomed to being one of the few
or the only physician of color in her class. Throughout her medical training
she'd rarely seen her identities reflected among the professional staff but
knew that she could readily find people who looked and perhaps sounded
like her among the hospital's food services and environmental services
staff. Sometimes she retreated to these spaces for respite.

Dr. Adebayo-Opeyemi knew exactly how to respond to her patients'
surprise when she introduced herself as their doctor. She knew to pause and
wait for them while they awkwardly set aside the meal-request cards they
had hurriedly tried to complete upon seeing her enter the room. She knew
to take a deep breath when they scanned the room for some external con-
firmation of her credentials—perhaps a nod from an approving white hospital staff member—if she was headed toward their medical chart. Along
with reading a chest X-ray and delivering devastating lab results, she had
honed these skills in medical school. Still, she was unprepared for the series
of identity-related aggressions (IRAs) she faced in this prestigious setting.
IRAs, a term we coined to remove the "micro" from microaggressions,
would come in all forms—from patients, fellow peers, and supervisors.

First, due to a misspelling of her last name in the hospital's system, Dr. Adebayo-Opeyemi was not able to begin the year with the other incoming physicians. Until the error could be rectified, she was locked out of the medical records she would need in order to care for her patients and complete their orders. Two weeks later, when she was finally permitted to start, her supervisors were frustrated that she was "just learning" to access the medical records and complained to the training director that she was not the "same caliber" as the other residents. In addition, she found that some of her colleagues struggled mightily to pronounce her name. Others barely attempted. Dr. Adebayo-Opeyemi, ever mindful of how awkward these interactions could be for her colleagues and patients alike, quickly granted everyone permission to "just call me Dr. Daisy!" Unbeknownst to her colleagues, however, in Nigerian culture an individual's surname is a source of great pride and significance. "Dr. Daisy's" father, Onye Opeyemi, had been a chief. Dr. Adaeze Adebayo-Opeyemi is a descendant of royalty. Her gesture of collegiality in the context of a seemingly simple clerical error had not only undermined a critical professional transition, but it also had begun to erode her sense of self and reputation in the workplace.

Mindful of the downstream consequences of her delayed start, Dr. Adebayo-Opeyemi vowed to work even harder to compensate. At times it was difficult to be totally present. A straight-A student all her life, she carried stress due to being behind, toxically compounded by frustration and sadness from knowing that some would attribute this to her race. She couldn't bring her full self to the workplace, so often it felt easier to shut down. Every time she was introduced by a colleague to a new patient, her muscles tensed as she braced herself and wondered, Is it going to happen again? Are they going to question my credentials? Dr. Adebayo-Opeyemi had to navigate numerous hurdles while waiting for the system to self-correct, which made it impossible for her to keep pace with her peers in the critical orientation phase of employment. Furthermore, those who would soon evaluate her job performance incorrectly attributed her delayed adjustment to diminished ability and formally recommended remediation.

## WHY THIS IS PROBLEMATIC

Dr. Adebayo-Opeyemi's experience illustrates how institutions that are ill equipped and under-practiced in working with individuals with a range of ethnic backgrounds (and other rising identities) can erect significant barriers to employee success. It's easy to see how enduring an environment like this could lead anyone with an underrepresented identity to shut down, lower expectations, and bring only part of themselves to work. Only a culturally humble and responsive setting would recognize that when Dr. Adebayo-Opeyemi acquiesced to asking staff to "just call me Dr. Daisy" and staff complied, they became coconspirators in the erasure of her ethnic identity. This is an extremely common occurrence, where individuals are urged to take on a Eurocentric name to make things easier for the privileged group. There is more on this in chapter 13, "Anti-Racism in the Workplace."

Identity-related aggressions such as these erode employees' sense of belonging in the workplace. Moreover, this pattern leads to increased emotional burnout, employee disengagement, and reluctance to bring one's full self to work. Ultimately, when a company isn't prepared to fully see its employees it loses growth potential, and this predictable cycle undermines both staff productivity and the bottom line. Speaking of productivity, why did it take so long to change Dr. Adebayo-Opeyemi's name in the system? Such obstacles will likely lead employees to seek positions elsewhere, which increases turnover, with the company incurring greater costs to onboard new employees. It also decreases staff diversity.

Dr. Adebayo-Opeyemi's experiences are not isolated events. Sadly, turnover in doctors of color is extremely common. Currently only 6 percent[1] of doctors in the United States are Black, which is less than half of the 13 percent[2] of people in the country who identify as Black—a crawling rise since 2003, when the percentage of Black doctors was 3.3.[3] Black doctors report problems in the industry, including lack of mentorship[4] and unsupportive (and at times hostile) work environments,[5] as illustrated by Dr. Adebayo-Opeyemi's experience. Increasing the diversity of our workforces will not only improve the clinical care that we provide, but it will also help build staff skills, practice, and effectiveness when working with people who hold a range of identities.

## WHAT TO DO ABOUT IT

Recognizing that Dr. Adebayo-Opeyemi's story is a microcosm of how institutions fail to fully see employees who hold underrepresented identities, how can we do better? How can we disrupt this predictable and costly cycle?

### *Stop making assumptions.*

Stop making assumptions about role and profession based on race (such as assuming Dr. Adebayo-Opeyemi was there to take orders for lunch), nation of origin, and ability status/disability. Stop making assumptions about sexual orientation and gender identity based on appearances. Stop making assumptions about socioeconomic status, for instance, or religion based on your own economic condition and religious affiliation or your experiences of those identities. Can you imagine a medical center, college campus, or law firm that challenges every member of the organization to suspend making all sociocultural assumptions about their patients, students, and colleagues? How might these settings be changed for those who have been historically underrepresented in these places? The beauty of this first recommendation is that it's something we can all do. We can all work to stop making assumptions.

### *Reducing assumptions, step-by-step.*

*Notice your assumptions.* The first step in reducing assumptions and stereotyping is mindfulness, becoming aware that you are making assumptions in the first place. Practicing mindfulness in these situations involves zooming in and taking a micromoment-by-micromoment view of our thoughts, feelings, and behavioral urges. What am I seeing, what am I thinking, what am I feeling?

Often, diversity trainings begin by naming common assumptions that we make or stereotypes we carry with us. For example, people who are Asian are good at math, a Black man in a hoodie is dangerous, a person with breasts identifies as female, people with disabilities are weak, and so on. While it can be uncomfortable (that certainly felt cringeworthy to write), it is important to bring the subscript written deep in our brains by society to the surface. Name it. Call it out. Admit it's there.

*Practice assumption mindfulness.* We can practice this awareness anytime, anyplace, related to any identity. Try it out walking down the street or through the grocery store. Try scanning your surroundings and asking, *Who do I see?* We naturally put people into categories in our minds: male/female, Black/Asian American, old/young. Notice how your mind sorts people into multiple categories.[6] This categorical thinking is hardwired into our brains. It's how we take in and process massive amounts of information, through mental shortcuts. While this subconscious streamlining—called "neural pruning"— is efficient, it also means we oversimplify. We create schemas about what it "means" to be of Indian descent, an immigrant, a trans* man, Muslim, and so forth.

Once you've noted the categories, get curious about the "and that means . . ." assumptions that follow. These will come quickly, as they are automatic. When encountering people you perceive to be "different" or "new," the "and that means . . ." will be loud and urgent. For the Asian American woman in her mid-thirties who perceives someone in the grocery store to also be a mid-thirties Asian American woman, the "and that means . . ." may be neutral or positive, such as "She's Asian and that means . . . she's like me," or ". . . she seems nice," or ". . . I'd like to know another Asian woman in my town." Conversely, when the same woman perceives a middle-aged person who is six feet tall with a strong jawline, thick hairy arms, makeup, a skirt, and long brown hair, the "and that means . . ." might be swift and furious: ". . . that person is transgender," ". . . they are brave to dress that way," ". . . they probably feel conspicuous and scared dressed like that in this town," or ". . . I should look away so they don't think I'm staring." Walking toward the checkout line, the woman perceives a young Black teen in a hoodie with his head down, walking quickly, hands in his pockets. The "and that means . . ." may be even louder, hardwired and accompanied by an accelerated heart rate: "He's Black and that means . . . he looks suspicious," ". . . he looks out of place in this upscale market," and ". . . where's my purse? It wouldn't hurt to take a step or two out of his way."

As you hone your mindfulness skills, you will recognize numerous assumptions that you make regularly about someone's identity, what you think that means about them, and how they relate to you and your safety. Next, try pausing to name the assumptions you've made: *"I called them male in my head," "My gut turned when they walked near me,"* or *"I felt anxious—I perceived danger. I backed away."* Pause to allow time for those assumptions to hang there in space, while challenging your assumptions: *"How do I know that they identify as female or male or trans\*?" "Where did I learn that Black men in hoodies are dangerous?" "What evidence do I have that this is true, in this moment, with this person?"* Pause to make room for other possibilities: *"Is it possible that the opposite is true?" "Is it possible that this Black teen is loving, trustworthy, and safe?" "Is it possible that the person I thought was a man based on body shape identifies as gender-neutral and uses they/them pronouns? Or has identified as a woman their whole life?"*

*Motivate yourself through empathy.* Pause to take the perspective of the Black teen who's tired from school and is trying to get in and get out with his groceries ASAP. Maybe walking into the grocery store always feels like parting the Red Sea as people bend away with their purses. I (Lauren) know that if I had grown accustomed to people moving slightly away from me clutching their purse or wallet, glancing out of the corner of their eye, I would aim for invisibility and efficiency. I might pull my hood up, avert my gaze, and walk quickly with hands shoved in my pockets. I know that I tend to withdraw from being fully present when I am walking with my wife in public. I resist the urge to reach out and hold her hand, stuffing my hand in my pocket instead. I might put a quick kiss on her shoulder, for fear of making other people uncomfortable. I have a limited circle of friends with whom I feel safe enough to lean over and hug my wife in front of.

Sometimes mindfulness is just too painful. As a result, the woman and teen never meet. These everyday, seemingly innocuous actions—identity-related aggressions—illustrate how acting out of our assumptions causes and maintains cycles and behaviors that keep us apart. Our actions cause people to feel shame because of who they are (this is called internalized racism/homophobia/sexism), and causes them to make themselves smaller—to act in ways that make those with privilege (white, straight, cisgender) more comfortable. These assumptions keep lines in place and keep us from learning to know each other.

### Say her name!

Once you have begun the (lifelong) process of building awareness, practice. Practice saying "Adebayo-Opeyemi." Say words, terms, pronouns, and names that might not come easily for you and learn to eliminate words, terms, and names of questionable and potentially offensive origin (see "A Few Tips to Go"). Expand the available range of morphemes and phonemes and language styles that your mouth can make. Find beauty in this learning. Even if you're offered a "Just call me Dr. Daisy" with a smile, learn the proper pronunciation of the person's name. Consider asking permission to write it down phonetically or record the pronunciation so you can practice on your own time. (Please don't ask them to keep correcting you while you stumble over it for five minutes, ending with "Oh forget it, it's too hard!")

### Use their pronouns.

The proper use of gender pronouns presents another opportunity to call someone "by their name" that's frequently missed or bungled by family, employers, and colleagues. Increasingly, individuals are coming out who identify as trans*, gender nonconforming, gender fluid, gender queer, and other identities on an ever-expanding list of gender identities and experiences. Perhaps a family member of yours has asked you to call them by a different name than you knew them by before or a new employee corrected you after you referred to them as "she," deftly saying in a calm voice "they."

For the vast majority of us, using new names and they/them pronouns is something we need to practice more. Yes, it's always been okay to use "they" in the English language, and we've been doing it all along when we don't know a person's pronouns. For example: "Someone left their sweater in the conference room; should we leave it so they can pick it up later?" Yet, when we are invited to staff trainings across institutions, employees often express thoughts such as these: "I can't get used to saying 'they'; it just feels wrong and awkward." "It's so hard to use he/him pronouns with that student; they look so feminine to me." "I have a hard time switching the pronouns I'm using for this person that just came out to me."

The good news is, there are easy ways to practice this in the privacy of your own home or with a trusted group, without adding the burden of your stumbling and practicing onto those who are already taking a risk by coming out. One of our favorite strategies is to dedicate one meeting a week (such as a staff meeting or morning recap meeting) where the goal is to practice using they/them pronouns for everyone, regardless of their gender expression (female, gender queer, male, or unknown). This way, the whole team can build mindful awareness and practice expanding the way they use the English language. The team members support one another by noticing how often "he" and "she" are used in conversation, helping each other in using "they" in the place of any he/she pronouns. Some groups have a bell in the center of the table that anyone can ring when "she" or "he" is used; others just say "they" in a medium volume, calling for the speaker to notice, quickly correct, and keep moving. This can also be practiced alone in the car (talk through who said what at a meeting that day) or with your family at the dinner table. After just a couple of hours of practice, using they/them pronouns fluidly becomes much easier than you'd imagine. And, like mastering a new language, doing it can feel pretty amazing! Another helpful tip: once you grow accustomed to using "they/them," you can default to using "they" in place of "he" or "she" each time you are unsure or have not yet asked someone what their pronouns are.

We can also make space for modeling that sharing pronouns is an acceptable practice in person or in text. Many college students have proactively begun introducing themselves by saying something like, "My name is Michael and I use he/him/they pronouns" to model gender inclusivity. Employee orientation nametags might include space for names and pronouns. It has become increasingly common to see pronouns included in professional email signatures and on business cards.

However, instituting companywide practices and standards related to gender-identity disclosure requires thoughtful consideration. For many, companies requiring the sharing of pronouns will be viewed as an inclusive and progressive move. But for those who are not ready to disclose their gender identity—because they feel unsafe, or are fearful of stigma or of professional or academic retaliation—a mandatory policy can be viewed as insensitive and a forced outing or closeting. There is no definitive all-or-nothing choice to be made here. Rather, we encourage organizations to be mindful of the complexity of these decisions and offer a guideline that we use in the practice of clinical psychology: all members of your organization will only feel as safe, seen, or included as your *least* safe, seen, or included members. Before committing to organizational standards, pause to consider, *How might this specific practice or standard impact our most vulnerable employees?* Ideally, companies should encourage those who feel safe and comfortable sharing their pronouns to do so verbally or in written text (on name tags or fashionable buttons, or in email signatures or on business cards). If someone does introduce themselves with their pronouns, respond with yours in turn—casually, not in a sarcastic or overly stilted manner. The goal here is to model that sharing pronouns is normal behavior.

When you mess up or need extra help, apologize and engage. When one of Dr. Adebayo-Opeyemi's supervisors first met her, despite several efforts (for example, immediately upon meeting Dr. Adebayo-Opeyemi, the supervisor asked for and repeated the correct pronunciation of her name and wrote down the phonetic pronunciation for her future benefit), the supervisor struggled to retain the name. Two weeks later she was embarrassed that, in part because she saw Dr. Adebayo-Opeyemi infrequently, she couldn't easily pronounce her name. However, instead of accepting her very gracious invitation to "just call me Dr. Daisy, everyone does!" her supervisor said this: "Thank you. I really appreciate your offer, and it might even be less awkward for both of us in the short term. I apologize that it's taken me several times to learn your full name, but I will. It's important to me that I say your name properly. I want to be able to introduce you with ease to people throughout our organization." This exchange demonstrates what individual practice can look like within an organization. As a senior leader, the supervisor was ideally positioned to model the importance of fully welcoming new employees. For more information and details on the apology process, see chapters 7 and 8.

Some organizations have begun to dedicate each month of the year to learning more about specific aspects of identity, such as race, religion, sexual orientation, or gender. This may sound like a painfully slow and somewhat arbitrary process; however, you will find that after several months of guided, intentional learning (supported by company emails, newsletters, dedicated web content, seminars, trainings, workshops, and dialogues), employees learn to engage in the process of continued discovery and commitment to cultural humility.[7] Be mindful of not focusing on the same three or four historic figures who are often celebrated—teach about new people to keep folks engaged. Once these core skills have been acquired, knowledge of specific content (which is endless across identities) becomes much easier to grasp. Again, it's a process, not a destination!

Even when we challenge assumptions and commit to the practice of learning about identities, we will make mistakes. When we do, it is necessary that we also learn to take the risk of apologizing. As a society we are in the early stages of learning to finally talk about subjects such as racism, sexism, ableism, and ageism. We are just learning to acknowledge and recognize the many forms in which the isms exist in and beyond the workplace. Many people are just easing into reading books like these. As these behaviors progress, our baseline skills in all of these areas—checking assumptions, practicing what's uncomfortable and/or new, learning to make sincere apologies—will continue to flourish not only across industries and in our professional lives, but in our personal relationships as well.

CHAPTER 3

# "PIONEERISM": THE GOOD, THE BAD, AND THE PAINFUL

· Seth's, Chris's, and Roxanne's Stories ·

*Seth, sporting his basketball team gear, was always the first to arrive at his philosophy class. That way, he could stake out his favorite spot in the front row where he'd have plenty of leg room and could easily interact with the professor. About a third of the way through the semester, one of the white teaching assistants approached him before class and with a furrowed brow asked, "Are you Nathaniel?" "No," Seth replied. While scanning the rear of the lecture hall, the teaching assistant muttered absentmindedly, "Oh. He hasn't shown up to my section once all semester. So, I thought he looked like you." Seth, who had attended every required teaching section, felt that familiar pang in his chest. He knew exactly who Nathaniel was—a white kid with dark hair who wore glasses and sat in the rear of the class.*

*When Chris, as a high school senior, took his seat in Advanced Placement molecular biology on the first day of class feeling motivated and proud, he recalls the greeting he received from the teacher. Glancing up from the desk at the front of the room, the teacher nodded and said, "This is AP molecular biology." It was more of a statement than a question. Chris sat in silence as the other students filtered in. After several minutes, the teacher walked over to where Chris sat, now joined by most of his classmates. The teacher repeated, "I'm sorry. This is AP molecular biology."*

*Although sleep-deprived from midterm exams, Roxanne was excited to join her family in Hawaii for spring break. Eager to get settled and comfortable before takeoff, she boarded the plane and stopped to store her Yale backpack in the overhead bin. She waited patiently while the young woman just ahead of her, who happened to be white, placed her luggage in the overhead before proceeding to her seat in coach. "Miss! Miss!" Was someone speaking to her? Roxanne turned around just in time to see the flight attendant quickly approaching. "Excuse me. The storage bins in this section are reserved for first-class passengers only." Roxanne's hand moved almost robotically to reach for the ticket in her pocket. Irrefutable proof that, unlike the white passenger just ahead of her, she was exactly where she belonged.*

These incidents are true stories that were told to us by individuals who share certain aspects of their identity. They are undergraduates. They attend prestigious Ivy League universities. They are student-athletes. They are African American and they are twenty-first-century "pioneers."

*v.* **pi·o·neered, pi·o·neer·ing, pi·o·neers**

*v.tr.*

1.

**a.** To venture into (an area) or prepare (a way).

**b.** To settle (a region).[1]

## WHY THIS IS PROBLEMATIC

Seth's, Chris's, and Roxanne's stories are all too common. They are examples of stereotyping; beliefs that Black students won't meet the academic rigor and expectations of the institution, that Black people can't excel in STEM courses or earn Advanced Placement class status, and that Black people certainly cannot accrue enough wealth to afford a first-class plane ticket. These stereotypes serve both to limit the role models and goals of African American children and erase the existence of Black people like Seth, Chris, and Roxanne.

These examples are often referred to as "microaggressions," instances where individuals act from biases that are enacted via words (such as saying, when meeting an Asian American person, "But where are you *really* from?") or actions (touching or clutching your purse or

wallet when walking past a Black man on the street) that serve to perpetuate injustice. In response to recent discourse by leaders of anti-
racism literature such as Dr. Ibram X. Kendi, founding director of the
Center for Antiracist Research at Boston University, we have shifted
our language from "microaggressions" and coined the term "identity-
related aggressions." While the "micro" once may have been a necessary "benefit of the doubt" to make the topic palatable for white
people to engage with, we and others in the field fear that the term
does not do justice to the profound, cumulative psychological and
physical impacts these moments have. Moreover, the acronym for
identity-related aggressions, IRAs, reminds us of the *compounding* nature and impact of these acts over time.

The aggressors in the above narratives may not have had relationships—teaching, friendships, professional—or exposure, such as
through the media or in literature, with African American and/or
Black men and women. Thus, they relied upon their socialized, ste-
reotypical schemas in these reflexive moments. Whether intentional
or not, their actions perpetuated these negative and damaging stereotypes and had lingering effects.

Being on the receiving end of these incidents (as "targets") is taxing and takes well-documented emotional and physical tolls. Citing
a few examples from a wide literature, identity-related aggressions experienced by high-achieving students have been shown to link to an
underestimation of perceived ability and higher levels of depression
and stress.[2] Identity-related aggressions can also be deadly, as they
have been linked to increased feelings of burdensomeness and, in
turn, thoughts of suicide.[3]

One of the most insidious aspects of identity-related aggressions
is that they occur without notice. They might sneak into a moment
where you're focused on something else, such as settling into class,
struggling to fit your bag into the overhead compartment while being
mindful of the passengers behind you, or rushing down the sidewalk
to meet your friend for lunch.

These unexpected incidents could leave you thinking, *Was that
about my race? That was messed up, right? Or am I overthinking it?*

Identity-related aggressions are inherently situated in historical privilege and power dynamics, such that the person who does the aggressing and inflicts pain is the one whose identity holds more power in society. Not only is the aggressor unaffected by the incident, they also are unaware that it even happened—a prime breeding ground for feelings of invalidation and erasure of the pain endured by those on the receiving end.

When you read the above stories, did you wonder or hypothesize about what happened next? Did you guess how Seth, Chris, and Roxanne responded to their aggressors? Sometimes we choose not to respond to identity-related aggressions. Chris may not want to point out the IRA because it could make his teacher uncomfortable. Embarrassing his teacher could be risky, as he is the one who will be grading Chris, and remember, he's already expecting Chris not to be up to muster. Thus, Chris might stay quiet for self-preservation. Roxanne might not want to make a scene and risk being labeled as the "angry Black woman" at the start of a long flight on which she will interact with the flight attendant regularly. Maybe she's just plain exhausted and this flight attendant isn't worth the energy it would require to speak up and educate her. Perhaps this happens every time she boards a flight and she folds it into the expected stress of flying, along with delays and turbulence. All of this is to say that if someone is not speaking in these moments, it is not because they are unaffected by the interactions. It is not because they didn't notice them, nor is it because they believe that these incidents are okay. More than likely, they're absorbing and swallowing the pain, maybe to process later, maybe to hold in forever. . . . Yet another incident to add to the vault.

Alternatively, Roxanne might respond immediately to the flight attendant. She might brandish her ticket, hurriedly saying, "I actually paid for a first-class seat, despite what you might think by looking at me." To borrow a metaphor from a popular YouTube video by Fusion Comedy, we can imagine identity-related aggressions as mosquito bites. Sure, you might expect to get one when you go outside (board first class as a Black woman). One bite is annoying, it itches, but it's a minor inconvenience. But maybe this is the tenth aggression

Roxanne's absorbed today, riding to the airport, navigating check-in and security, using the lounge, boarding her flight: a compounding series of race-based traumas. Maybe she's covered in mosquito bites while fellow passengers sit comfortably sipping their coffee. This bite might be one too many. As a result, Roxanne might express anger and hurt, might draw the attention of other passengers. Someone observing this might feel she's overreacting and think, *It was a misunderstanding but did the flight attendant really deserve to be confronted?* But the passenger has missed the hundreds of bites Roxanne's sweater hides, which illustrates the painful paradox of the "angry Black woman." Others see overreaction and lack of emotional control, when in reality Roxanne is likely much more practiced in emotion regulation and processing anger internally than the white onlookers.

Experiences like these, and many throughout this book, are what we call "the break of the wave." Across the United States and around the world, employers and universities are increasingly aiming to diversify their teams and cohorts across many aspects of sociocultural identity. This is the wave, which we think is spectacular. However, there are pain points that accompany being part of the wave.

Remarkably, the pain points experienced by Seth, Chris, and Roxanne haven't evolved much across the generations. In many respects they still hold "pioneer" status. Like the first Black people to integrate a classroom, lead a battalion, or hold an elected office, they are still treated as anomalies. Society still questions whether they belong. When the student/wave breaks against historically white spaces, moving sand and creating space for new learning and new schemas to develop (for example, Black students can be the smartest in the class), it hurts. It's painful to be the surprise; to be questioned amid your existence; to be interrogated about your belongingness. To be the wave is to have to prove yourself and reshape the minds of those socialized not to expect you, again, and again, and again. A single wave that reaches the shore, like the pioneer, must be fierce and formidable. Without reinforcements, however, it will become absorbed along the shoreline and one might question that it ever existed. This is why pioneer status is so dangerous.

Renowned Georgetown coach John Thompson, after winning the National Division I Men's College Basketball Championship in 1984, was asked how he felt about the "amazing achievement of being the first African American to win the title." Coach Thompson bristled at the question. To paraphrase, he said, "I take offense at the notion that somehow I'm the first African American with the intelligence, dedication, and skill to achieve this title. Many others of African American descent could have accomplished this goal had they only been afforded the opportunity to do so." By calling out the obvious racial disparities in his profession, Coach Thompson rejected the pioneer crown. Never one to mince words, we imagine him having said, "Yes. I'll take the title but you can keep the crown."

When accepting an award from the Anti-Defamation League, its first African American recipient, then Massachusetts governor Deval Patrick recalled a poignant exchange that he'd had with former Virginia governor Douglas Wilder. When speaking about his pioneering status as the first African American governor of a US state since Reconstruction, Wilder famously said, "Being the first will only matter if there is a second." Prophetically, Patrick became the second. And now there have been two. Period.

Consider what Seth "the pioneer" observed about his experience as the first African American student from his high school to attend Harvard: "There are so many talented and brilliant students from my high school in Columbus who belong here, too. It's not enough that I'm the only one and it hurts not to have them here." To be perfectly clear: no one wants to be regarded as a pioneer in an arena where they should be one of thousands. A thousand waves will reshape the entire landscape. They bring a force that cannot be discounted.

Fortunately, these waves are rising all over the country. College student racial, ethnic, and socioeconomic demographics are more diverse than ever before. Universities are aiming to hire more diverse professors by whom students can be inspired while seeing themselves reflected in the academy. Higher education institutions have argued for the superior quality of a diverse education all the way to the Supreme Court. Again, this movement is a great thing. But if we are to learn anything from the experiences of Seth, Chris, and Roxanne, we must make the break less painful. We who have the power and privilege must be willing and prepared to absorb more of the shock so that these students are free to focus on being students.

## WHAT TO DO ABOUT IT

*Learn your schema.* There is much we can do as individuals to anticipate and increase the efficiency of this movement. A big part of the work is preparing your own mind for the waves to hit. First, assess the ways in which you have to make space in your brain for new possibilities and new learning. Of course it can be hard to gain awareness of what you don't know but there are some steps you can take.

Begin by imagining your colleague is telling you a story about how their neighbor was kind enough to help them load a couch into their truck as it started to rain on Sunday. Recall the last time someone told you about their doctor giving them good news. Imagine a friend complaining about the CEO of their company taking monthlong trips to Hawaii while they have a measly ten-day vacation allotment. What did the helpful neighbor look like? What did the intelligent doctor look like? What did the jet-setting boss look like? If you're anything like me (author Lauren), they all look white, male, and able-bodied. None of them was gay, Indigenous, or in a wheelchair. Just like the people around me growing up, they looked like me. When I am told about an intelligent doctor, a brilliant boss, or a strong and helpful neighbor, some part of my brain tells me that they are male and white. What images came to mind for you? Whatever images presented themselves are likely your "normal," the schemas that you were taught to expect. Every time I hear a medical story, I have to pause to notice that a white male doctor has come to mind. I have to ask myself why I didn't imagine the doctor as Black. Why wasn't she in a wheelchair? Why didn't she have a Spanish accent? Pausing to intentionally change out the people in the images is a helpful strategy for pushing the sand aside so that new schemas are allowed to enter. These schemas are also referred to as implicit biases, or subconscious stereotypes—assumptions or behaviors that are automatically triggered when we perceive people's identities. Implicit biases are well researched and show that we have immediate responses that we do not even recognize, such as associating an image of a Black person with "criminal" and a white male with "doctor."[4]

Unfortunately, we cannot "unlearn" the implicit biases that we have acquired throughout our life. Instead, we must accept that they exist, build mindful awareness of when they happen, aim to reduce the amount that they impact our behaviors, and work to build new neural pathways alongside them. In short, this means assessing the implicit biases you hold (using the exercises below and tests available online); learning to pause when you perceive someone's identity to check for implicit biases—for example, when someone is driving poorly in front of you, do you assume that they are female, ederly, or Asian American?; acknowledge that bias and where you learned it, if you can remember; and take time to generate new possibilities (for example, my implicit bias suggested someone was a female when they could, in fact, be male). We have expanded on these tools below and throughout this book.

Try a reflection activity with pen and paper by making a list. What types of people were you primarily around growing up across identities such as race, sexual orientation, religion, socioeconomic status, nation of origin, and Indigenous heritage? As a kid, who did you invite to your birthday parties? With whom did your family celebrate special occasions? What did they look like? Where were they born? What did they believe? Does this list reflect who came to mind in the first exercise or who you frequently see holding powerful roles in the media? Both? Neither?

Next, write a list of identities that were *not* common in your town/city/school. Include categories like gender (trans*, gender nonconforming), Indigenous status (Native people), sexual orientation, religion, disability, and socioeconomic status. Consider that second list for ten minutes and then answer the following: What were you taught about these groups? What are your assumptions? What stereotypes do you carry with you? Write it all in the margins and don't hold back.

This part may be challenging because we often conflate stereotyping others with being a bad person. Do not be ashamed or embarrassed here. We all have stereotypes embedded deep within us, and the more assumptions and stereotypes you can name, the better chance you'll have of correcting them. Recognizing the schema you have will help you catch your brain making split-second judgments when you are passing the Black teen in the grocery store with a hood over his head or when you turn to the Asian American person in the room to ask, "What's 20 percent of a $189 check?" Review and acknowledge this list. See if you can remember where you learned these ideas and commit to making space for new learning. Allow these teachings to be inaccurate. In other words, question them by asking, "Do I have any personal experience that supports that theory? Do I have any evidence to the contrary? In which category do I have more evidence?" Commit to curiosity and to being uncomfortable. Look forward to meeting people who do not fit your previously held molds and expectations. Enjoy and embrace the surprise.

At the organizational level, leadership can engage in a very similar process. Organize a meeting with qualified external trainers or take time to self-reflect on the following questions: What is the history of how identities have been represented in this organization? Which identities are represented at each level? Are people of diverse identities evenly distributed throughout? Were they ever? What defines a leader here? As a leader in this organization, what assumptions and stereotypes do I hold about leadership potential? Who do I see "at the top" when envisioning the future of the company?

Of course, organizational assessment needn't be subjective and most organizations have quantitative demographic data that can be analyzed. Make no mistake about it: if you decide to move from a homogenous to a more inclusive organization, the entire system needs to prepare for the waves to hit. Whether you are a senior leader of a university, an investment firm, an airline, or a professional sports organization, the system, *your* system must first acknowledge its history. As the American novelist James Baldwin said, "Not everything that is faced can be changed, but nothing can be changed until it is faced." The system needs to be primed to understand its biases, to make room for new possibilities, and to have its expectations broken.

In each of these student examples there are a multitude of ways that the student, the aggressor, or a nearby bystander could respond. Individuals finding themselves in each of these roles could likely benefit from skill building. We revisit Chris's, Roxanne's, and Seth's stories in chapter 10, "Responding to Identity-Related Aggressions."

*Learn the "two-step."* As with all skill development, offering a single or even periodic bystander/ally training for your workforce on how to be more culturally aware and responsive when you hold privilege won't suffice. We recommend learning the "two-step," and, yes, it's like learning to dance. For a whole host of reasons, many organizations will insist that the recommendations from training X, no matter how carefully selected and adapted, simply "won't work in our culture." We've witnessed this repeatedly. All good dancers must be ready to skillfully guide even their most reluctant partners across the dance floor. Consider priming trainees/employees by saying, "No training will be perfect for our unique culture and organization. You can expect that will be the case today. However, as you engage in the training, wherever you see misalignment, think about how you would enhance the approach so that it hits the mark for our community. Our collective goal is to learn these evidence-based skills and make them work for our organization. This will require open minds and creativity but, since we're known for our innovation, we should be able to manage." This important step will encourage staff to see bridges in place of barriers and eliminate potential and unanticipated obstacles to implementation. This is step one.

New skills need to be practiced with regularity to become accessible when needed, especially in emotionally charged situations. The Multicultural Psychology Consultation Team (MPCT) at McLean Hospital/Harvard Medical School begins every meeting with individual reports of upstander moments both seized and missed in the prior week. The term upstander is based upon evidence-based bystander intervention and training originally used in institutions of higher education to prevent sexual assault and racial, homophobic, and transphobic harassment. Bystander training teaches observers to take personal responsibility for intervening in these problematic situations. In MPCT meetings, one might share that "On Monday, a senior clinician on my unit was talking about a patient who uses a wheelchair and said, 'He's just trying to get attention. I saw him walking just fine without it.'" The MPCT member might go on to say, "I didn't say anything in the moment, and I feel ashamed about that. I was scared to put off my boss since I'm pretty new." Or "I said, 'Actually, that patient has congestive heart failure, so while their legs might look fine to you, they can become dangerously out of breath and have difficulty getting around without the chair." Or "I didn't say anything in the moment because I know this clinician would become reactive and defensive, but I do want to address it with them privately. Can you help me come up with a response?" This simple practice raises awareness of the prevalence of identity-related aggressions and opportunities for intervening; promotes skill building and group problem solving using upstander behavior and skills; and promotes individual and systemic change. Challenge your newly trained staff to develop and share their strategies for embedding newly acquired skills into the organization's routine meetings, failures, successes, and missed opportunities alike. Celebrate people for sharing and engaging in the conversation openly. Reward departments for implementing innovative approaches that work within your company's culture and structure, as these will be the most effective and enduring. An external consultant can teach new skills but cannot prescribe how best to apply and integrate these skills into the fabric of your organization. This second step will help staff to seize ownership of the skills by making them their very own.

Finally, when integrating upstander or allyship training into the organizational culture, anticipate staff pushback. When we conduct workshops, we almost always hear some version of the following: "It's fine to practice being an upstander in this workshop. But in the real workplace, this is scary and can be really hard to do." We have to be honest. Yes, it can initially feel terrifying to be an upstander. But you'll find that just as with any other skill, it gets easier with practice over time. Be prepared to validate and encourage staff by sharing that some coworkers have to face these moments of temporary anxiety and fear daily. Emphasize that being an upstander develops empathy, which will help them grow and also make the company more equitable, just, and successful.

As you aim to make more diverse social and professional connections across identities, know that you are going to keep making mistakes. This is inevitable. We, you, all of us often continue to act out of our assumptions, even when we're trying hard not to. So you might finish this book, wake up tomorrow with the best intentions, and then still hurt or offend someone—whether it's a colleague, a stranger, or someone you care about. Recognize that the goal isn't perfection. Rather, a commitment to continual self-interrogation and effort is what's required.

# CHAPTER 4

# BECOMING "EXPERTS"

Sometimes, being "the first" in a workplace setting can morph into a brand-new role. Invariably, once an employee with a rising identity is seen as knowledgeable about issues of identity and inclusiveness, some leaders and colleagues will start to pay attention. As trust grows, leaders will become more receptive to the recommendations and observations made by said rising employee and agree that, come to think of it, changes must be made! They are ready to take up the torch of justice and equity. Next, leadership will pass that torch . . . right back to the rising employee, knighting them with the role of "diversity expert" and assigning them the responsibilities. This is what happened to us (the authors) and what, nonetheless, led us toward what became an extremely fulfilling and inspiring journey. We have grown to appreciate our platforms and truly value the experiences that brought us together as friends, colleagues, and ultimately coauthors. However, our initiation in these roles was challenging and highlights a common phenomenon that organizations should be mindful of.

### • Stephanie's Story •

*I was fortunate to have earned my "stripes" in higher education administration within a system that valued student activism and inclusivity. The Division of Student Affairs at the University of Michigan (UM) launched*

*the first LGBTQ Affairs office on a US college campus back in 1971.*[1]
*UM installed gender-neutral bathrooms decades ago, and welcomed Jewish students when other institutions of higher education would not. UM also created the model for intergroup relations and dialogue. It was far from utopian, but staff development of the 1,200-strong Division of Student Affairs workforce, under the leadership of Dr. Royster Harper, was grounded in principles of social justice.*

On my first day on the job, a colleague plopped down in my office and asked matter-of-factly, "So, how do you identify?" The year was 2000 and I was completely taken aback. I'd never been asked that question before and didn't even know how I was supposed to respond. I don't remember my exact words but I'll never forget my thoughts and feelings in that exchange. The learning curve here is going to be a steep one—no one taught me about identity in graduate school. And yet, I felt safe and eager to explore this new professional culture.

My title was associate dean of students. My portfolio included Critical Incident Management and Specialized Student Services, which comprised Counseling and Psychological Services, Services for Students with Disabilities, and Sexual Assault Prevention and Awareness. Fundamentally, to do this or any job effectively within the DSA, all staff, from leadership to student employees, had to be willing to answer the basic question my colleague (and director of the LGBTQ office) posed to me on that first day.

"How do you identify?" reflected a stance. Like taking an oath, those four words were code: People here are committed to a never-ending process of learning about our own, each other's, and our students' identities. I would also soon learn that if I meant to excel in this role, I needed to consider the intersection of those identities within the context of my designated areas of expertise. Finally, I needed to be brave enough to act on that knowledge. Indeed, it was a steep but exhilarating learning curve, and in full disclosure, I screwed up plenty along the way. In my six-year tenure at UM, critical incidents arose involving every aspect of identity, including disability (specifically mental illness), race and ethnicity, national origin, sexual orientation, gender, and religion. Learning to respond to these incidents—controversial campus speakers, *fires, deaths, natural disasters, hazing, stalking—from a multiculturally informed perspective alongside my colleagues was humbling, heartbreaking, and life-changing.*

Six years later I landed in a new professional setting, this time in academic medicine in the Boston metropolitan area. I had been recruited to the new role—to create a comprehensive hospital-based college mental health program—in part because of my cumulative academic, administrative, and clinical expertise in college student mental health. The new institution and surrounding community were more racially segregated than what I left behind in Michigan and seemed less adept at navigating differences. Geographically, I was closer to my hometown of Philadelphia, but socioculturally I felt even further away than when I was in the Midwest. I was homesick in a way. Homesick for integrated neighborhoods and huge, festive, cultural gatherings—both staples in the sections of Philadelphia I knew so well. I was homesick for Italian ice and cheesesteaks and Jewish delicatessens, all Philadelphia favorites. I was homesick for my family. I found myself in what I had named the "social justice time warp"—the experience of going backward in time, or regressing in terms of social justice perspective and inclusiveness. And I had been in the time warp before. I attended graduate school at Vanderbilt University, in Nashville, Tennessee, in the 1980s. Even before the first day of class, I got to file a housing discrimination lawsuit. Excited to see an apartment near campus, I showed up and was told it had "just been rented." Suspicious of the timing, I asked my white friends to view the same listing and they were immediately invited to sign the lease. The social justice time warp crystallized later that fall when Black students at Vandy protested a longstanding campus tradition: Old South's Day, a celebration in the land of Dixie of how things used to be. Try to imagine white undergraduate students dressed as southern belles wearing voluminous petticoat dresses and waving Confederate flags. It was surreal.

The Boston area was not Nashville circa the 1980s, but the contrast between the setting I had left behind in Michigan and the new one was unsettling. My new colleagues were brilliant, accomplished, and devoted to patient care. But it was clear something fundamental had changed. In this new workplace, people didn't speak openly about being gay, Muslim,

*Latinx, white, or Black. They didn't use words such as "identity," "racism," or "inclusivity." In late December, Christmas wreaths appeared in the halls and Christmas carols filled some offices—overt displays of the majority's religious symbols, to the exclusion of others' symbols and customs, something I had explicitly been taught not to do. I identified as a cisgender woman, meaning I identified with the same gender that I was assigned at birth. I identified as African American, straight, and Christian. I held privilege in multiple categories of social identity, including socioeconomic status, religion, education, national origin, and sexual orientation. Objectively speaking, I was succeeding in my new role and thriving. But, over time, I felt increasingly isolated and conspicuous.*

*I quickly learned to wear my credentials at all times. When I walked onto patient units, I learned to introduce myself in an authoritative tone: "I'm Dr. Pinder-Amaker." Otherwise, staff could appear startled, abruptly asking, "Can I help you?" as if I had made a wrong turn. If I entered the hospital grounds to find that my parking lot was closed for the day except for professional staff, I could watch the cars ahead of me with white passengers getting waved through without being questioned. I, on the other hand, could count on being stopped by security to show my credentials. One day I joined a team of colleagues to propose a research project involving college students and patients. In our small group of six, another program director, who was white and male, anointed me "the diversity expert"! I was both flattered and confused. Did that just happen?! How did I earn that honorific? And why not "college student mental health expert," especially since I was the only one at the table with college student mental health expertise?*

*Sometimes the Did that just happen?! moment occurs with the realization that a shift in workplace responsibilities has coalesced into a new professional identity and set of expectations. I entered this new setting well versed in the burdens inherently faced by a Black professional working in a predominantly white institution. These professional burdens are well known to employees of color and include but are not limited to being called upon to represent the Black and/or minority experience as a monolith; becoming a de facto support to both colleagues and trainees who are repeatedly on the receiving end of identity-related aggressions and* identity- and race-based traumatic stress; serving as the minority presence on a multitude of committees; and being labeled as "the diversity expert" regardless of qualification, all while fulfilling the role for which one was ostensibly hired and striving to meet criteria for promotion.

I was recruited to McLean Hospital because of my college mental health expertise to develop the hospital's first comprehensive college mental health program. Over time, however, my portfolio in student mental health was expanded to include being "the diversity expert." I came to develop a complex, ambivalent relationship with the label. A few years ago, I took stock of my institutional roles relative to DEI and was alarmed to find I was serving in leadership roles on eight committees and task forces throughout the hospital and the Partners HealthCare system. These commitments were in addition to the dozen or so local, regional, and national college student mental health committees I was serving on at the time. How did that happen?! To be clear, I valued this work. I was proud of my and my colleagues' efforts and of the advances that had occurred within my institution in the past decade. I was finding my social justice voice in this new environment and leadership was listening. Had I not rolled up my sleeves, found wonderful allies, and pitched in, I could not have survived. Yet, like so many, I was not being compensated in salary or title for this difficult work, which I had embraced at considerable personal and professional cost. Eventually I came to believe that continuing to assume this role, in this manner, was also hurting my institution. I wrestled with my own complicity. I had enabled a system I care about to claim that it "values DEI" without properly resourcing and valuing the heavy lifting that is DEI work. There simply must be a better way.

▪ Lauren's Story ▪

As a white, cisgender, able-bodied, queer female of European American descent who grew up in a small homogenous town, I had a lot to learn about diverse identities and the impacts of holding marginalized identities. I was fortunate enough to complete my graduate training in a program that had a strong social justice mission. In our classes, research meetings, and interactions we had a shared goal of bringing identities into the room via open, direct dialogue. I had difficult conversations; I messed up; I attempted to repair; and I learned more than I ever thought possible.

Flash forward. It was the first day of my third-year clinical placement in 2014 at McLean Hospital. Immediately upon entering the clinic, I started smiling, shaking hands, introducing myself, and accumulating data. I initiated that involuntary scan . . . is anyone here not straight? I calculated where I should position myself along a continuum of options. At one end of the continuum was the decision to never share my sexual orientation. At the other end was the decision to live openly and without restriction, freely sharing with my new coworkers any aspects of my identity that felt relevant. The research question for the data at hand? What is the evidence for and against the safety of coming out as queer? The aim of my "study" was to take a scientific approach to predict the unpredictable and answer the question: how would things at this job change if I told people I have a wife? Let the inquiry begin!

Like any trainee I was sure to make multiple administrative and clinical errors, and initially my presence would be experienced as a net negative in the clinic. Coming out while being a net negative to the team might further amplify my deficits. If coworkers and staff felt uncomfortable about my sexual identity, tolerance of my bumbling, anxious, trainee status would be quickly exhausted. One point for staying in.

Later, on the first day of my final training year, I ascribed the label of "probably not straight" to one of the senior members of the team, admittedly based on stereotypes related to the clinician's mannerisms. With a bit of additional sleuthing I confirmed that, indeed, they were not straight. However, in addition, they were not out in the workplace. Identifying a staff member who, despite possessing seniority status and power within a hierarchical organization, was not out sent a clear message to me as a trainee: it's not safe here. I had entered a social justice time warp.

Seeing my wedding ring, people asked about my "husband" and how we'd spent the weekend. Each and every time, my stomach dropped. Did I dare to share accurate details about my personal life knowing that doing so would unravel existing expectations and frameworks my coworkers already held about me? Dare I disclose that my wife and I had explored the

*Berkshires mountain range, knowing that doing so would embarrass the supervisor who had just inquired about my husband? That probably would not be great for my performance evaluations, which were pivotal for my future as a psychologist. Another two points for staying in.*

*My head was filled with so many conflicting thoughts: coming out would definitely mean a loss of privilege. But coming out might also grant me more leverage to make changes. I could trust in the relationships I was cultivating, opt to disclose my identity, and gain immediate credibility that my voice was worthy of being heard: I could express that how we approach LGBTQIA+ issues with patients and among our workforce needed to change. I might be able to make this clinic safer for LGBTQIA+ patients. I might be able to improve the quality of care.*

*Across each clinical setting I entered, I eventually built up the courage to come out. It was not because I ever felt "safe" or supported per se; more because otherwise I did not feel genuine and I felt angry that I was not comfortable bringing my full self to the workplace. I began with my supervisors, weaving my sexual orientation into the conversation somehow—sometimes at work, sometimes at conferences or during happy hours. I had a little fun slipping "my wife" into a story about the weekend, observing the slight shock, then pausing while "recalculating, recalculating . . ." scrolled across their faces. I fake-smiled through the "random" follow-up stories, told to make me feel at ease, about their gay cousin, who was "just amazing," and who I "would just love." I sighed through the monologues of how appalled they were about the current political situation, followed by the requisite "Well, at least things are so much better now for gay people." I cringed through the awkward trailing off of some conversations and slumped through the letdown of coming out to a gay senior colleague who had minimal to no response—singlehandedly dashing my hope for that golden nugget of affirmation, a high-five, total acceptance. Still, some folks surprised me by jumping right in to suggest we go on a double date, saying they would love to meet my wife, and treating me like any other colleague. That felt affirming.*

*What came next continues to surprise me. In each of these settings, I had an immediate increase in the number of LGBTQIA+ patients I was assigned. My peers started consulting me about their LGBTQIA+*

*patients. I was asked to present a seminar on the range of ways people might identify related to gender, which led to three more talks on other units. I was just a novice therapist; how did that just happen? Seemingly overnight I'd been knighted the LGBTQIA+ expert. This conferring of expert status presented another dilemma. While I did not regard myself as an LGBTQIA+ specialist, I did know that I would be compassionate, accepting, and culturally humble toward such patients. I did know some of the professional and casual LGBTQIA+ lingo. I did know I was comfortable exploring connections between identities and mental health symptoms due to practicing throughout my doctoral training. So I worked to earn expertise status, leaned into the growing demands of the organization, and never protested. While it was complicated, I did build an appreciation and passion for this role, found deep connections to peers with similar values and experiences, and, because of the "expert" designation, made measurable change throughout and beyond the organization.*

## WHY THIS IS PROBLEMATIC

As you may have picked up through our narratives, there are many reasons why designating a person with a rising identity as a "diversity expert" can be problematic. First, such experiences are not unique to academic medicine, but can be observed in virtually *every* industry, profit, and nonprofit. An organization's receptivity to change is likely correlated with how long it has committed itself to hiring diverse leadership and invested in continued learning and education. Second, assuming someone is a "diversity expert" of any sort because they hold a rising identity simultaneously involves stereotyping and ignores the level of training required to be such an expert. Being married to a woman does not automatically come with a brain download showing Lauren how to navigate the world as a lesbian or, for that matter, as a gay man, trans* woman, or nonbinary employee. Being Black doesn't confer special knowledge upon Stephanie about the vast and diverse experiences of Black people or all people of color. We do not automatically possess knowledge about how gender, racial, and sexual identities interact with mood, how to repair conflicts across difference, and how to increase resilience. We might be assumed to be "safe" by other folks with rising identities but this is also not a given. In fact, these assumptions can be dangerous and costly to your organization in myriad ways. When we look for employees to increase the cultural awareness and knowledge of our workforce, we should look at their credentials, not simply their identities.

Further, accepting the torch of educating and training one's colleagues, peers, and supervisors on topics related to identity can be a professional risk. Engaging in conversations related to such topics as race, gender, and ableism[2] is, by nature, uncomfortable. Being the person who is perceived as adding more discomfort to the workplace can risk one's work relationships, reputation, opportunities for promotion, and job. For example, as the first employee who uses walking assistance in the form of braces or a wheelchair, you might be asked to provide training on ableism in the workplace. While some coworkers might look forward to your talk and value learning more about the topic, many will be confronted with their privilege and likely by things they have been doing wrong, such as not asking a visitor if the stairs are accessible for them or being ignorant of reasonable workplace accommodations in their state. This may conjure feelings of embarrassment or shame, and these coworkers may become defensive. Colleagues might feel resentful or nervous about being in your presence—worried that every behavior is being viewed under a microscope and every comment is being judged.

In addition to the professional risk, assuming the role of "diversity expert" can be incredibly exhausting. As illustrated in both of our stories, underrepresented minorities are frequently asked to do this work in addition to their demanding, full-time jobs. The negative physical and psychological correlates of discrimination are both well documented and cumulative. Moreover, gaining more knowledge about identities can make it easier to recognize micro- and macroaggressions in the workplace, and gaining more knowledge about one's positionality can make it easier to recognize your own mistakes. Also, the isolated "diversity expert" may not have anyone with whom to process these new insights, thereby exacerbating feelings of loneliness and anxiety.

From the outside it might appear that Stephanie and Lauren were passionate about this work and eager to fill the educational void. But for both of us, our efforts were spurred on by passion mixed with duty. Having formerly learned in environments rich with people discussing and navigating identities and difference, we had entered the social justice time warp in these new positions. We were adjusting to (relative) identity deserts where we were managing full-time jobs while navigating daily identity-related aggressions relative to our identities. We were observing and feeling all of the identity-informed interpersonal conflicts in our midst. While holding underrepresented minority status, we were called upon to do painful and, at times, impossible work. With every request, we had to measure our desire for growth and change against the professional risk that accompanies that change.

And what about that term, "diversity expert"? You may have noticed us putting it in quotes. What does "diversity expert" mean, anyway? While we both were trained in academic institutions steeped in awareness and education related to identities, that was not necessarily what we led with when we began working in new settings. Rather, we focused on the tasks for which we were hired, but eventually we were asked to do this work based on how others perceived our identities (Black, queer). We said yes because we were informed and passionate about this work and cared about the organization. However, we were not hired into roles designed, resourced, or positioned within the institution to catalyze change. Our on-the-job training to become "diversity experts" was inspired merely by existing within systems that needed help and possessing the personal experience to inform that work.

Tapping internal resources to fill this need can initiate a perilous cycle of events. First, identifying someone as an "expert" related to identities (which we all possess) sets up a detrimental and unhealthy dynamic in which some employees are perceived as the problem, while others are viewed as the solution. Second, relying upon existing personnel for this heavy lifting absolves institutions of properly resourcing this important and demanding work. Too many institutions claim that they value diversity but don't invest one extra dollar toward realizing that goal. Third, this unfair burden excludes genuine diversity, equity, and inclusion expertise from entering and informing the system while designated "experts" struggle to adapt. Additionally, these pioneer experts often hold lower-level positions in the organizational hierarchy, positioning them with little authority to make change but with high occupational risk. Finally, when designated experts depart in search of more affirming and healthier environments, organizations flounder and regress as they cope with the loss and attempt to understand what just happened.

### WHAT TO DO ABOUT IT: CULTIVATING THE ORGANIZATION'S EXPERTISE

Breaking this cycle requires resources and commitment. It is important that hiring decisions be specific and intentional. If your organization desires the benefits of a more diverse workforce, excellent! Recruit and hire accordingly. If your organization aims to increase the cultural awareness and humility of the workforce, hire professionals who are trained to facilitate this challenging work. Consider bringing in external expertise instead of jeopardizing the well-being and careers of the very people recruited to improve your organization. By properly investing in this work, you demonstrate to your employees that you value organizational growth, the diversity of the workforce, and having a culture that is both multiculturally informed and sustainable.

When tapping internal expertise, value the work in tangible ways connected to compensation and/or promotion. Just as faculty at a university may opt to teach fewer courses and focus some of their energy on writing, research, and earning awards, offer a similar reduction in workload, a salary increase, or a stipend for professional development to employees who assume these responsibilities. If we haven't communicated our point effectively, then let us state it plainly: *this work is extremely painful, deflating, and draining, and people should be compensated for it.*

Motivating your organization to strive for inclusive excellence is a never-ending process that requires expert navigation at the helm. Think of it as a voyage that the entire system takes together. Everyone must pack for the ride. Along the way, you'll discover that you neglected to bring necessary supplies. To forge ahead, the successful vessel will pause to pick up these resources —to gather more supplies (for example, in the form of training, new policies and practices, and organizational restructuring) and assist others who might be struggling. Over time, some seasoned travelers, especially your designated experts, will grow weary of this process. It can be too slow, frustrating, and demoralizing. Others will choose to disembark because they don't like the destination as it comes into view. That's okay. The ultimate goal is to be able to navigate these rough waters while permitting diverse talent to thrive along the way. For this to happen, your travelers must be carefully nurtured and sustained throughout the journey. To be clear, being an active member of the crew is everyone's responsibility. This book can serve as a practical traveler's guide. If you are feeling compelled to serve as a designated expert for your organization, there are important factors to consider. Chapter 12 details specific strategies for sustaining yourself, wherever you might be on your organization's journey.

Practically speaking, what does it look like when an organization moves away from the "designated expert" model? First and foremost, Diversity, Equity, and Inclusion strategies and interventions will shift dramatically from a focus on individuals to a focus on systems. There are clear steps your organization can take to signal that this cultural shift is underway. First, it's imperative that organizational leadership make a full commitment to creating a workplace that promotes cultural awareness and humility. Full stop. In so doing, it's important to communicate that this commitment is *everyone's* responsibility, not the work of a few. Every member of the organization will have a role to play in advancing these efforts. We know there is a trickle-down effect when leadership commits to this work; it models bravery, safety, and job security while approaching something that can be intimidating and anxiety provoking.

When leadership commits to creating more just and equitable organizations, anticipate that some staff will feel overwhelmed and anxious, while others will feel that these initiatives are long overdue.

Wherever staff fall along this continuum, it can be reassuring to hear that the organization's efforts will be continuous. In other words, when an institution commits to striving for cultural awareness and humility, there is no final destination. Rather, all members are committing to a continuous process of learning. Further, organizations should expect that, even though you're on a well-intentioned path, employees across the identity continuum will find aspects of your efforts problematic and hurtful. When criticism is expressed, it is important that leadership pause to listen, reflect, and let defensiveness come and go before responding—more on this in chapter 8, "Leading by Empowering Listening."

*The three pitfalls.* Next, priorities should be institutionalized through the formal processes and structures that anchor, define, and guide the organization, including strategic plans and values and mission statements. Organizations that are new to this work should be especially mindful of three common missteps: (1) solely designating experts from within the organization; (2) further marginalizing the marginalized; and (3) tasking underrepresented employees with disproportionate expectations and responsibilities. Here, we provide three corresponding examples of skillful navigation around these predictable landmines.

First, prevent building or maintaining a culture that solely designates experts who also hold other roles in the organization. Hire the expertise needed to advance this work. Companies are better off hiring a diversity officer or creating another role designed to continuously bring new education and training into the organization. Hiring an employee for this leadership role sends the message that you value this work with your dollars. Having a dedicated person or group carrying out this work also increases its quality, as budgeted positions can be dedicated to continuing education, content development, and company-culture-specific dissemination. Further, a person hired to do this work can focus on being an educator and mediator without needing to balance this against other roles like, say, coeditor, supervisee, and friend. We cannot stress enough that this is the way to go. In addition to having ample time and space to dedicate to this effort, the diversity officer must be given adequate power within the organization to make change, must be outwardly respected by leadership, and must have the necessary funds to perform their role. Posting an underpowered diversity officer is like placing a single balloon at the front desk announcing the new initiative. You need support and resources for a comprehensive movement to take root.

If and when you do tap internal staff, be fully prepared to compensate and support employees who assume responsibilities beyond their job description and workload. Returning to Lauren's and Stephanie's stories, a more informed supervisor might have said, "I am wondering if you would like to take on a more formal role reshaping the culture of our workplace. If this is something you are interested in, I would like to know what we can take off your plate and in what ways we can compensate you for this role, which is likely to be complex and taxing. Please take some time to think about this, and know that we are not expecting you to take on this role, but rather offering it." Know that this employee is going to have an increased social burden in addition to the increased workload. This employee is likely going to have to choose between their bread-and-butter job security/advancement and the advancement of the cultural humility/learning of their organization. Take it from us that this is an agonizing choice to make on a daily (sometimes hourly) basis, and employees who do so deserve an increased salary or a decreased workload.

Second, elevate, amplify, and centralize the people, places, and practices charged with promoting diversity, equity, and inclusion. There is a longstanding pattern of institutions of higher education establishing multicultural centers in remote campus locations with subpar conditions. If your campus had such a center or Black house, can you picture it now?

Nearly fifty years ago the University of Michigan officially opened the original Trotter House, a Black student cultural center named in honor of William Monroe Trotter (1872–1934), who was an African American journalist, real estate businessperson, and advocate for racial equality in the early twentieth century.

Like many of these designated spaces on campuses throughout the country, the original Trotter House was located in a repurposed, "rambling old house" situated on the outskirts of campus.³ In 2019, the ribbon-cutting ceremony was held for the unveiling of the new Trotter Multicultural Center. Trotter 2.0 is located on the main avenue at the center of campus, a stone's throw from the highly trafficked student union. Trotter 2.0 is an elegant architectural structure designed for inclusivity. Students can *literally* see themselves and each other reflected within its interior walls, as mirrors are interspersed among the portraits adorning the walls. Today, the Trotter Multicultural Center works to enhance multicultural awareness across campus and is a place where students, faculty, staff, and alumni can hold meetings and events.

In a similar nod to student activism, the University of Michigan was home to the nation's first campus-based LGBTQ office and provided gender-neutral bathrooms more than twenty years ago. In 2002, amid an escalating national climate of discrimination and hate targeting Muslims, the university opened conveniently located prayer rooms to accommodate Muslim students' increased needs to pray multiple times daily. These efforts inspired increased designation of sacred places across campus to accommodate the religious and spiritual needs of students of all faiths.

The contrast in structures and evolution of purpose and function are powerful illustrations of what it looks like when an institution moves from marginalizing the marginalized to prioritizing multicultural excellence. Similarly, when we recruit and hire the necessary experts to skillfully promote multicultural excellence, these roles are often buried deeply within organizational charts, with limited visibility and authority. As demonstrated by the unveiling of Trotter 2.0, these positions should be ranked among the institution's leadership, with authority for and oversight of systemwide efforts. This structure increases the likelihood that efforts and resources are visible, coordinated, and disseminated throughout the institution.

In 2010, McLean Hospital initiated a strategic planning process for redefining its organizational values. The senior vice president of strategic planning convened a hospital-wide Core Values Committee to engage the community in this important, multifaceted effort. I (Stephanie, one of two managers of color in the organization) was not a member of this committee, but learned from a colleague that the members had curated the organizational values to a semifinal list of ten core values, among them teamwork, innovation, excellence, and compassion. Perplexed and disappointed to learn that diversity did not make the cut, I appealed directly to the committee chair by writing a letter, which included these excerpts:

> First, I want to thank you for the work you've done in narrowing the field to 10 possible values for our organization. In response to your survey requesting feedback and input, I'd like to submit, for your consideration, that we include the value of "diversity." I understand that it was discussed briefly and dismissed, at least in part because "we are not diverse." I beg to differ.

> Please consider our entire community as it relates to gender, sexual identity, religion, ableism, socioeconomic status, culture, race and ethnicity. I'd suggest that not only are we diverse, but as the number-one-psychiatric-institution-in-the-US, we might . . . envision a McLean Hospital that one day models how to effectively engage in difficult dialogues; how to work and live in an inclusive community in which staff and patients feel safe to openly identify as "gay, bisexual, transgender, disabled, Muslim, privileged" and so on; how to become better clinicians, coworkers and managers because we recognize the value of our diversity in the workplace. I believe that we owe it to each other, our staff, and our patients to begin this difficult work in a more intentional way.

Key aspects of the vice president's response were highly effective and instrumental in cultivating the organization's expertise. First, she contacted me immediately to gain a deeper understanding of my concerns. Next, she asked permission to share the appeal letter with the president of McLean and with the Core Values Committee. Finally, she invited me to join the committee meeting during which the appeal letter would be discussed. I agreed, and throughout the process, I felt that my concerns were heard and considered at every level of the organization. That was validating and I felt hopeful. The members of the Core Values Committee were appreciative of the shared perspective and proposed that I cochair the committee going forward.

Even better was how the VP responded to the suggestion. She said, "It sounds like we all would welcome Stephanie's expertise and leadership. However, she already has a full-time job and it wouldn't be fair to ask her to assume this additional responsibility. We can invite her to join the committee; however, I'll continue as chair in my role as the vice president of strategic planning to lead this important effort." That moment solidified my commitment to promoting the hospital's efforts to become more inclusive and multiculturally informed. I welcomed the invitation to join the committee and especially appreciated that I wasn't asked to hold the weight of doing the work. For the organization, that moment sent a very clear message to the workforce: this work would be everyone's responsibility.

In the span of ten years, McLean would establish a hospital-wide Committee on Diversity and Inclusion, LGBTQ+ and Implicit Bias task forces, an LGBTQ+ Employee Resource Group, and a Dimensions of Diversity group dedicated to ongoing staff education and training. In 2020, McLean hired its first chief diversity, equity, and inclusion officer (CDEIO) and announced an Anti-Racist, Justice, and Health Equity task force. The CDEIO is a permanent member of the organization's senior leadership body and reports directly to the hospital president. Both efforts are resourced, formally incorporated into the strategic plan of divisions within the hospital, and enjoy the full, public support of the hospital president. Today, we (authors) are proud to support and lead these efforts, Stephanie as CDEIO and Lauren as senior adviser to the Anti-Racist, Justice, and Health Equity task force.

# CHAPTER 5

# THIS WORK IS NOT LINEAR

· Lauren's Story ·

*In the final year of her social-justice-informed doctoral program, a white student named Lauren attempted to take action by pressing leadership to improve support of their students of color. She teamed up with a mentor of color and another white graduate student and, together, they crafted an email to all of the students who might be interested in joining the cause. Students were encouraged to complete a survey documenting issues that they had witnessed or experienced in the program. Mindful of not wanting to burden the students of color, the threesome attempted to do some of the heavy lifting. They prepopulated the survey with experiences they had heard from students of color over the years, thinking it would be easier for students to simply scan and select from among the curated list of egregious incidents. They spent a few hours drafting the email message and, when it was ready, hit "send."*

*Soon after, Lauren received the first reply. It came from a friend of hers who was a student of color in the program. As Lauren eagerly scanned the message, she felt her heart skip a beat. Lauren's friend expressed that they were having "strong reactions" to the email, especially this line: "There is a feeling that some faculty take students of color in order to meet the program's social justice initiatives, without providing support and knowledge necessary for a non-oppressive learning environment for POC in their labs or mentoring." A few other friends replied that they agreed. For some, the sentence reflected a tone reminiscent of white students' complaints about affirmative action policies. As the realization sunk in, her face reddened and her stomach twisted. Somehow, Lauren had miscalculated and now she would have to face her classmates at the next meeting.*

*Walking down to the second floor and feeling mortified, Lauren steadied herself. She turned the corner, took a deep breath, and walked straight into the classroom. Knowing that she had hurt her friends, she made a point of looking them in the eyes. She owed them that.* At least I can have the courage to make eye contact, *she thought. Not being able to apologize and address the email error until after class was torturous. Lauren couldn't stop reciting the lines of the carefully constructed email in her mind. She couldn't stop wondering,* How could I have messed up so royally? How, after five years of being in this intensive program aimed at increasing my cultural awareness and humility, could I have created something that hurt people that I care deeply about?! *As the minutes ticked by, the worst-case scenario suddenly occurred to her.* What if, even after class ends, my friends don't want to talk? What if they never *want to speak with me again? Lauren feared she had dissolved the deep trust that they had built over the years and worried that she had permanently damaged the friendships. She felt nauseous.*

*The email chain went on for days. Some students were deeply hurt. Some found the email helpful. Some wanted to talk about it and others didn't. Eventually, a student of color proposed a meeting to discuss how the now-lengthy email thread had impacted their community. Lauren was humbled by the willingness of her colleagues to meet and share their feelings with her, the person who had hurt them.*

### LOSING THE THREAD

Perhaps you guessed that the "Lauren" in the story was me (author). The passage of time has helped me reflect on this situation with greater clarity and appreciation. I would be lying if I said that I had immediately accepted the gift of education from my peers graciously and moved on as a new, improved, and enlightened version of myself. Instead, I was in a constant state of turmoil inside and I felt like giving up. Looking back, I recall feeling envious of my white peers who hardly ever seemed to engage in this work. They seemed to remain safe on their "island of good terms." I, on the other hand, was the source of hurt, anger, sadness, and contention, and had jeopardized my friendships because of it. I wanted to be back on the island of good terms with them. It was comfortable there. I felt sad and adrift and considered stepping away from the mission altogether. If "crawl into a tiny ball and disappear" had been an option for how to spend my final semester on campus, I might have chosen it, despite it not being in line with my values.

### FINDING THE THREAD

In preparation for writing this chapter, I revisited this difficult episode and searched my email history for the original thread. I secretly hoped I wouldn't find it and worried that reading it could undermine the confidence I would need to finish this book. Eventually I did find the dreaded email, but what happened next was completely unexpected. This time around, with the benefit of perspective and objectivity, my experience of the exchange was dramatically different. What I saw now were two white students (aided secretly by a mentor of color) attempting to do a good thing. The letter was a deeply thought-out message in which they had acknowledged their positionality. They had written that the email would likely not be ideal and expressed their hope that they hadn't misrepresented what needed to change in the program. The white students' friends responded that they were having reactions to the text, especially that last line. Many of the students of color agreed. The white students reacted with upset feelings and asked their peers of color to "call [them] in" as white people as opposed to "calling [them] out." While calling-out includes public statements like "That didn't feel right and I need to tell you why," calling-in is typically in private and opens the door to a dialogue: "I'm wondering what you meant when you said _____." The students of color pointedly explained that by working against societal expectations to remain silent and instead sharing their genuine reactions, they had invited their white peers in. The students of color had taken risks by speaking out and trusting their white peers to be able to hear and accept their feedback. They had trusted that after all this training their white counterparts would understand the importance of, and be equipped to hold some of, their pain. As the writer Ijeoma Oluo explains,

> If someone confronts you with your privilege from a place of anger or even hatred, if someone does not want to take the time or does not have the emotional energy to further explain to you where your privilege lies, know that this is still a kindness. Try to remember that the alternative to not being made aware of your privilege (no matter how it may sting) is your continued participation in the oppression of others. Someone is giving you an opportunity to do better, no matter how unpleasant the delivery. Thank them.[1]

Revisiting the chain after so many years made it all much clearer. In focusing on my own shame and embarrassment, I simply had lost the thread. My desire to be the perfect white ally placed the focus on me. On my abilities. My failings. My reputation. My tunnel vision made it impossible for me to see that my friends *were* calling me in and they had done so in the most honest and vulnerable way. Rather than absorb the hurt, silence themselves, or overprepare an email protecting my white feelings, they took the greatest risk of all and shared their raw emotions. What could have been more trusting and courageous than that? Looking back, I am in awe of it. My feelings, even those of shame and regret, are important *and* they are secondary. This experience taught me more than any other, and I continue to learn from it. Going forward, I will aim to focus more on gratitude for the gift of feedback. I will aim to wallow less and stay more present.

## WHY THIS IS PROBLEMATIC

Making the commitment to becoming more culturally humble and responsive means just that—it is a *commitment*. This work is not amassing a series of check boxes. There is no final destination or deadline. There is no straight path to follow. Lauren does not one day become "competent" or "certified" to navigate the workplace inclusively as a white person. Stephanie does not suddenly get "unquestioned admission" into queer spaces without hesitation or being tested, no matter how earnestly she has worked or how much she wants to be a safe straight person. This work is both a value and aspirational, a horizon that one is always working toward. Forward movement requires consistent reflection of one's own identities and the ways they interact with the identities of others. Forward movement also requires seeking to understand the experiences of each historically underrepresented or rising identity, a list that will continue to shift and change over time.

To be frank, this work is hard and can be painful and draining. Once your eyes begin to recognize the intricate system of marginalization, power, and privilege that has always surrounded you, you will feel a heaviness, which at times can be overwhelming. This well-documented process often has been compared to taking the red pill from the film *The Matrix*. Once you take the pill and begin to see historically primed power dynamics, you cannot unsee them. You will see these dynamics everywhere and within every interaction. Once you can see the suffering associated with levels of oppression (societal, institutional, interpersonal) experienced across the entire range of sociocultural identities (such as race, religion, sexuality, gender expression, and disability), you will feel waves heavy with discomfort.

Although no two people have identical *Matrix* pill reactions, there is a set of common uncomfortable emotions. If the aspects of identity that are most important or salient to you are associated historically with barriers in your country, you might feel angry, gaslit, sad, and overwhelmed. For example, taking a class on race in America as a person of color may not teach you more about your daily experience, but it might make you think about it on a deeper, systemic level, linking to history what you were never taught in school and bringing your emotions closer to the surface. If, however, the aspects of identity that are most important or salient to you are associated historically with privilege in your country, you might feel guilty, sad, overwhelmed, and hopeless. For example, taking that same class as a white person will likely mean not only learning the disturbing truth about our history, but will also bring you in touch with the deep, heavy shadow of racism and how it still infiltrates our society today, hurting people you care about and those you haven't yet met. You will go through surprise, awe, disbelief, defensiveness, sadness, and pain. All of these feelings are perfectly valid. It is valid to feel angry and gaslit when oppressed and marginalized. It is valid to feel sad and hopeless about unfair and unjust systems that have been in place for centuries. The key is to tolerate the emotional discomfort while learning the specific actions we can all take to eliminate interpersonal, institutional, and societal oppression.

Once you habituate (as much as anyone can or should) to the pain that accompanies this enhanced and heightened awareness, there will be pain in trying. It's painful to make mistakes when trying to do the right thing. To illustrate, here are workplace missteps shared by individuals who described themselves as "fairly experienced" in doing this work.

Kyle, a gay, white, cisgender male and expert "Safe Zone" trainer, routinely forgets to check his privilege at the door, talking 60 percent of the time in meetings when there are women, trans*, and colleagues with disabilities and other rising identities present. Manuel, a straight, Latinx chief diversity, equity, and inclusion officer, didn't think to check in on his gay friend following the Pulse nightclub shooting.

Both Kyle and Manuel described experiencing spirals of anxiety once they learned of their missteps. They expressed thoughts like "I can't believe I missed that; I really suck at this work." Like Lauren, they felt urges to withdraw, to hide out and hope people hadn't noticed their mistakes. A common workplace response is to become hyper-focused on task completion and to avoid interacting with a hurt colleague. However, this will likely only pause your discomfort, as avoiding the targeted colleague will likely only lead to reinforcing the cycle of oppression in the workplace. Moreover, the resulting distress may be even greater when you (someone committed to promoting justice and inclusion) are the perpetrator. Your colleague may be left to feel even more invisible, and may be left to wonder, "Did that really just happen? Was that about my race/gender/ability status/ nation of origin? Or am I being oversensitive?"

## WHAT TO DO ABOUT IT

*Recalibrate your definition of progress.* If you are lucky, people with different identities and experiences will see or experience your mistakes and decide that you are worth the time and energy to educate. Working hard to be hyperaware, engaging daily in actions to undo your socialization as an oppressor, and then graciously receiving the feedback that what you just said or did was really hurtful represents progress. The thing is, being your natural/socialized self (if you hold privilege in a space) is likely to be oppressive or marginalizing in some way, so you are bound to mess up. So get ready to hear that you're messing up. In fact, you'll probably get more negative feedback the longer you do this work, as more and more people will trust you enough to give you this feedback. As soon as you realize you're being given feedback, pause your action, focus on listening, and be mindful of any defensiveness that might be starting to bubble up. Hint: defensiveness is the faithful companion of the thought "But that was not my *intention!*"

*Invite and accept the gift of feedback.* Early in this work you may well feel the urge to correct the person giving you feedback, reassuring them that you never intended any harm by your statements or actions. This defensiveness can shut down a dialogue quickly. Remember: it is not the *intent* that matters, it is the *impact*. Regardless of where you are in this journey, by engaging in this work your goal is likely never to cause harm, but to create a more just and equitable world for all people. Accept that despite your good intentions, and despite what you've learned about undoing all of your socialization, you will, at times, impact others negatively. The process of undoing years of socialization is a never-ending unraveling and reconstructing. Of course, receiving feedback on how you are hurting others while striving for inclusivity feels much different from a critique of your inconsistent tennis backhand or less-than-stellar winter driving skills.

Feedback in this arena often feels deeply personal and stirs strong emotions such as guilt, shame, anger, sadness, and frustration. Ideally, as you move along this journey, you will also experience increased gratitude. Try responding quickly: "Thank you for giving me that feedback. I really appreciate you taking the extra time and effort. Thank you for trusting that I can receive it. I will reflect on what you have shared."

*Don't expect banners and balloons.* Also, unlike most skill development, improved ability to communicate across differences and through difficult dialogues does not come with the same type of acknowledgment and mutual high-fives. As Ijeoma Oluo so aptly put it, "You are not doing any favors, you are doing what is right." For those accustomed to improving skills from a privileged space, it is common to expect reward and celebration. You've always been treated as special! Initially, it can feel awkward to become more skillful in doing this work with little positive reinforcement. It's like nailing a triple axel in the dark.

All of the above factors make it hard to sustain this commitment. It is easy to feel burned out when you have messed up a few times in a week, when your work is not recognized and largely scrutinized (by people who do and do not share this value), when you are putting emotional labor into bettering the world and . . . no one says a word. Ideally the rewards will come through more genuine relationships and witnessing the growth of those who hold privilege around you. It might take a while for your colleagues to celebrate with a "thank you."

*Persist.* Hold tight; keep doing the work. Persistence and sustaining yourself through this work are specific skill sets. Further, you must acknowledge and maintain your own boundaries. You do not have to take on every training opportunity or teachable moment to educate another person. Instead, engage when the opportunity feels in line with your values and emotional reserve. Engage in self-care to recover and recharge. Seek comfort, processing, and further learning in affinity spaces where people share your identities (such as a Black professionals group or a meeting about processing white privilege). We will discuss these and additional strategies for building persistence and resilience in chapter 12, "Sustaining Yourself." For now, take heart and know this: if you persist, the rewards will come. (See the "Enjoy" section below for a glimpse of future possibilities.)

*Celebrate.* Celebrate yourself—privately. Do not celebrate yourself on social media, bragging about how many Black Lives Matter protests you attended this year. Don't post that selfie of you and your Black friend so that everyone knows you have one if you don't post pictures with friends regularly. Instead, journal or take note of your learning process. Notice and celebrate internally how you are getting better at using they/them pronouns, or how you asked the interviewee if they would prefer the elevator or the stairs regardless of how they appeared to you. Notice that you're getting better at refraining from sharing every idea you have in a meeting. Celebrate moments when you acknowledge your own failings, take pride in your growth, and trust that your continued education is making a difference, even if no one is telling you it is.

Celebrate other people's work—publicly. Celebrate people with different identities by using your power and position in the organization to lift up their voices or suggest they receive increased compensation for this work. Cite people by name in your work. Share your appreciation of their work in meetings or other public forums. Celebrate people acknowledging that you see them doing the work. Be aware of urges to feel competitive with others who hold the same privileged identities, and note tiny feelings of excitement or relief when they mess up. Rise above those feelings and reinforce the things they do well: "I think it's really amazing that you received that feedback so openly and are working hard to do better. I find that inspiring as I know I sometimes lose steam when I mess up." Offer yourself as an affinity space to process difficult feelings: "I know this work is hard. As a straight person who has worked for years to become an effective ally, I still make mistakes. That's something we should really just discuss together as straight people. I am always here if you want to talk, process, express, or problem-solve together." Relatedly, if you find yourself shutting down and feeling jaded, this could signal that it's time to reach out to someone who shares a similar identity to yours who is also committed to this work.

*Enjoy.* There's a reason we're motivated to do better in this work. It's not just that healthy, diverse workforces do better work and improve the company's bottom line. Having friends with different experiences, perspectives, holidays, and decorations is fun, humbling, inspiring, and encouraging. We (authors) cannot wait for the first time Lauren can take Stephanie to a drag show. Lauren loves enjoying the art on Stephanie's walls, which is so different from what she grew up seeing. It feels special to be trusted. Far and above the pain of doing the work, the red *Matrix* pill brings a technicolor view of a once sepia-toned world. It feels like seeing many deeper, more beautiful, and intricate levels of the world. Once in a while you can lean back into a relationship and laugh hard, connecting for a few moments, forgetting the histories that attempted to keep you apart, finding a friendship or a creative collaboration that you might otherwise have missed entirely.

# CHAPTER 6

# MOVING THROUGH THE FREEZE

## · Malik's Story ·

*Having polished his presentation, Malik, an accomplished African American neuropsychiatric researcher, was confident in his ability to secure a six-figure donation from the Brain Matters Foundation for his lab. The gift was such a high priority for the university's capital campaign that both the university president and the vice president of development joined to support and facilitate the ask. Ten minutes into the small-group meeting, it became clear that the agenda would not be followed. The foundation chair, an amiable older white man named Charles, interrupted frequently and dominated the meeting with multiple off-topic anecdotes. Then suddenly, when describing a character from one of his stories, he exclaimed, "and this man was Black!" Charles then turned directly to Malik (the only person of color at the small table) and added, "I mean . . . blacker than you."*

*Charles paused for a moment. Malik thought, "Oh, he caught himself. Here comes the apology." Instead Charles continued, "Well, you're not really Black, I suppose." Silence. The VP deftly redirected the discussion and Malik resumed the presentation. Eventually, the formal request was made and well received. Malik had succeeded. Along the way, however, things had gone terribly wrong.*

*Shaken, Malik retreated to his office and continued to process what had just happened. After ten minutes there was a knock at the door. "Come in." It was the VP, who breathlessly said, "That was incredible!" She had* heard it too? Thank goodness she's coming to debrief with me. *"You were wonderful. We're going to get the gift. Great job! This is a huge bonus for the hospital and a real feather in your cap. We couldn't be happier."* In the weeks that followed, the incident was never acknowledged.

We have all witnessed or personally experienced events like these. What you feel and think during and after likely is affected by your positionality. If you are Black, it's personal. If you are a person of color who is not Black, it's relatable. If you are white and observant, it's painful to watch.

## WHY THIS IS A PROBLEM: RECOGNIZING THE FREEZE

No matter how you identify, if you felt your stomach drop or had a sense that something wrong was said, it is likely that the following internal process was set into motion. First, you might ask yourself, *Did he just say that?* Then, you may look around the room to check for other reactions. What are the other people in the room thinking? Things may slow down as you become hyper-attuned to the moments as they are unraveling, like you are watching a train crash. This feels so wrong; is someone going to say something? Should I say something? Is it safe to say anything? What would the costs be to me, and others, if I said something?

If you are in Malik's shoes you know that what happened is not okay and can readily describe why it is wrong. You also know that speaking up could cost you and your team the important (and needed) donation. Further, addressing Charles's comment in the moment could cost you your job or increase tension and weaken relationships at work. Charles holds a great deal of power in the room, and unfortunately that usually takes precedence.

As a seasoned professional, Malik might decide that the safest thing to do in the moment is to maintain a neutral face (smiling might be safer, but it feels disingenuous and has the long-term potential of reinforcing Charles's behavior). As a midcareer professional, it is likely that Malik has amassed a repertoire of go-to skills and behaviors for coping with these types of incidents. He could try to connect to his self-worth, strength, and pride in being a member of the Black community and remain focused on the next section of his presentation. Over time, however, Malik might notice a gradual shift in his response to the freeze, which represents a mounting dilemma: as his coping skills are honed and perfected throughout the early stages of his career, his patience and motivation for accessing them may wane as he matures and advances. Why? The impact of these incidents on Malik (on his thoughts, feelings, and memories) is cumulative. No one else in the room can know the cumulative weight that he carries into the presentation and must take with him when he leaves.

In an ideal world, the company or team would have undergone extensive identity-related training and have protocols and policies in place so that if Malik chooses to speak up in the meeting, Charles is prepared to manage his defensiveness, respond with appreciation, apologize, and move on, hopefully a little wiser. Sadly, exceedingly few teams are in that place.

If you are a white observer in the room, maybe your skin crawls and you feel queasy. You may recall Malik talking about comments like these in the past, or you might remember reading an article about colorism or shadeism, the treatment of those with lighter skin as "closer to white," ascribed both some privilege as well as rejection from the Black community. You might think, *This is that moment, the moment someone is supposed to say something if we want things to change in this world, in this workplace—I'm white, and I have relative safety, I should be using some of my privilege for good. But what if I make everyone else more uncomfortable? I don't even know what to say to articulate how this is wrong, and does Malik even want me to say something? Would Malik appreciate me pointing this out in this moment, or would he be uncomfortable with more time and attention spent on Charles's comments?*

We call this "the freeze." It can last for seconds, minutes, even hours. Despite your internal rush of thoughts, an outsider would likely observe you sitting still, quiet, maybe looking around the room or staring at your notepad. The freeze is dangerous because although the room may be filled with allies and advocates, the observed silence and inaction can be painful for the target and convey that this type of behavior is okay.

Of course, it's often *not* safe to say something. In our experience, the offenders are usually those who hold mostly (or all) privileged sociocultural identities, including positions of power in the workplace. In these moments, we believe the responsibility is on those who hold a little more privilege than the targets of these statements. In this example, white employees are in a unique position to intervene and with less to lose, though most people will fear speaking up due to risk of losing power, status, or adding stress to interpersonal dynamics. This is a delicate skill requiring practice.

### WHAT TO DO ABOUT IT: MOVING THROUGH THE FREEZE

You may have noticed that the vice president took action in this example, moving through the freeze. After Charles's second comment, she deftly redirected the conversation. This is an important skill to develop for those in leadership or organizational positions, as they have the power to change the topic and shift the attention from someone in Malik's situation. In an ideal scenario, the VP would have recognized the marginalization happening and taken manageable missteps. She would have noticed that the topic was uncomfortable, identified that Malik was the target of an identity-related aggression, been aware that this event likely triggered a physiological fight-or-flight response in Malik—heart racing, speeding thoughts, increased anxiety, fear, or discomfort—and recognized her ability to afford him some time to recover and refocus. She could have been even more helpful by asking questions of others in the room to take some attention off of Malik temporarily. The VP recognizing and enacting her power could have been an act of compassion and allyship.

As someone with relative power in the room with respect to race and role, the vice president has the positionality to stop Charles and recommend that he not continue. She could tread lightly, saying, "Okay, let's stop there and refocus on the task at hand." If the VP feels secure in her position and upsetting Charles is not significantly risky for her role, she could acknowledge the moment more directly by saying, "I think we should stop here; I don't think that is an appropriate way to talk about race." Likely, however, she will be nervous about embarrassing and upsetting Charles. We are trained to keep the privileged offender comfortable and safe. If we call them out, we risk our own standing in the company and might be passed up for a promotion in retaliation. It's safe for us to keep those in power safe. In this case, the VP might choose a middle path by speaking to Charles one on one afterward and sharing her own experience of the meeting. She might pull him aside and say, "The comments you made about race in the meeting made me really uncomfortable and I think conveyed a message that reflects negatively on your foundation." Notice how she is talking about her own thoughts and feelings instead of assuming how Malik felt and making that the focus. The alternative approach—"I think you hurt Malik's feelings"—puts even more burden on Malik by fueling stereotypes of weakness, oversensitivity, and anger. Moreover, making herself the focus increases the likelihood that Charles will act from *his* emotions and approach Malik with an apology.

What could Charles possibly have been thinking in this moment? As a white person in the United States, he might have been raised (consciously and/or unconsciously) to hold racist and shadeist beliefs. Despite the common if misguided adage "I don't see color," Charles was likely prompted to think about race during the meeting when he noticed Malik's race. Charles's brain, like all human (and lizard) brains, took in the room upon entering, looking for patterns and anomalies. Consciously or not, his brain noted "white, white, white, Black, white," and probably "man, man, man, man, woman." This initial scanning, which we all do, brought race to Charles's mind, which may have triggered his comments. But why say such things? Of course, it is possible that Charles was acting in an overtly racist way, trying to undermine Malik's pitch by bringing up race to make him uncomfortable and throw him off. It's also possible that Charles was not intending to act in a marginalizing way, even though he did inadvertently. If we give Charles the benefit of the doubt and assume that he didn't *intend* to marginalize Malik, then the explanation comes down to pure and simple socialized-as-white-in-the-United-States, combined with lizard brain.

Charles might have "woken up" halfway through his comments, felt a little uncomfortable, and experienced a skin crawl or a mini-freeze. Perhaps he thought, *Oh, no! I just talked negatively about race in front of a Black person! I know, I'll just make sure they know I'm not talking about* them! Charles's behavior is a classic example of "that wasn't my intention." Still, he could have self-corrected in a number of ways. First, he could have been more honest and transparent: "Wow, I don't know where that came from," and then asked the vice president, "Can you get us back on track?" If Charles had been brave and practiced, he could have apologized in the moment: "I'm sorry, that was inappropriate to say." He could have avoided some of the comments altogether if he had been able to reset earlier. Importantly, if you find yourself in Charles's position, we recommend that you pause, acknowledge your mistake, and move on quickly. Apologizing profusely may burden Malik further by putting him in a position of having to describe how he feels, which it is likely not safe for him to do, and to "forgive" Charles in front of the whole group.

### BEGINNING TO THAW

After the freeze, the meeting likely will continue, and people will part ways and resume business as usual. Those with awareness that something "off" transpired in the meeting will slowly begin to "thaw" or process what happened. Some may initiate deep processing and not be ready to talk. Others might seek out a trusted colleague to process, text a friend, or chat with a spouse or roommate at dinner that night. Still others might "forget" the incident entirely until much later when something triggers the memory.

Regardless of your processing style, the commonality is that these moments end up resounding for days, months, years, and even decades. By pausing to consider how these effects accumulate over time, it's easy to appreciate the exhausting snowball effect of marginalization. For example, Malik will likely flash back to this memory each time he pitches for a big donation, maybe even every time he walks into a predominantly white room. Of course, Malik has long been the target of shadeism. However, Charles's comments were multifaceted. Was Charles insinuating that it is *good* that he is not perceiving Malik as Black? How perplexing it is to have your racial identity simultaneously be marginalized (Charles insinuating that being Black is bad) and attempted to be stripped from you ("Well, you're not really Black, I suppose"). What does it mean that Malik's colleagues remained silent? Is silence what's expected in this environment? As Malik begins to thaw, he may continue to wrestle with these and other questions.

The good news about the long-term impact of these events is that there are many times, places, and ways to intervene. You can intervene by sharing your feelings about what happened, using "I" statements and being mindful of not trying to add stress to those already burdened. You can also intervene by being supportive of the person who was affected by the comments. You can intervene and disrupt this predictable pattern by giving someone a knowing glance or sending a a simple text like "Did that just happen?!" If you're new to this work, you may try reaching out to Malik in an email starting with "I wanted to share my thoughts on what I experienced in the meeting. I am not expecting a response but would gladly discuss this further in person if you would like."

By simply acknowledging the event you can validate that marginalization exists and communicate that "Yes, that just happened. It was not okay. It was not just in your head. You are not being overly sensitive." By offering support you can communicate, I am opening the conversation. I am saying, "I am here to listen if you would like to vent. I am willing to take steps to be a more effective advocate going forward." Perhaps Charles reflected on his comments and realized they were wrong. There are many ways that Charles can repair the damage (we offer examples in this, and the following, chapter), but the most important way, regardless of your positionality, is to acknowledge these events—despite our training not to. We need to learn to notice the freeze happening and practice taking the opposite approach—moving through the freeze—either during or after identity-related aggressions. In the cognitive-behavioral-therapy world, we call this "opposite action," noticing our mood-driven urges (freeze; stay silent, aka safe; and withdraw), and choosing to do the opposite (speak up, redirect, reach out).

Finally, if you hold power or privilege in an organization, it is critical to acknowledge inappropriate identity incidents, even after the fact, directly with the target. Lack of recognition is even more distressing for those on the receiving end and, although you may not have the awareness or the skills to intervene in the moment, inaction will lead to the disillusionment and departure of talented professionals like Malik.

CHAPTER 7

# WHEN YOU'VE MESSED UP

· Miguel and Aleph's Story ·

*It was February 2020. Miguel and Sleph, both middle school English literature teachers, were out for an evening stroll in New York City when something bizarre and unsettling happened. Having lived in their Upper West Side neighborhood for six years, their routine was rehearsed—a two-to-three-mile walk, ice cream at their favorite family-owned bistro, followed by a magazine and book tour through their local Barnes & Noble. They carried their laptops, as they enjoyed lounging in the bookstore while working on lesson plans. Something about being surrounded by familiar literary works with the scent of coffee and freshly baked cookies wafting in the air inspired their determination to engage their seventh- and eighth-grade students in the classics. The middle school years can be challenging for their students whose interests frequently shift from an impassioned love of literature and creative writing to science or math. Hoping to amplify Black voices during Black History Month, Miguel and Aleph moved through the aisles in search of titles that would resonate with these prepubescent kids. Later, they would debate who had been first to see the prominently placed book display and let out an audible gasp. They couldn't believe their eyes. Was this some sort of joke? A beautiful banner hung above the elaborate display. It read, "Barnes & Noble celebrates Black History Month!" Just below were elegantly arranged volumes. They scanned the display, taking it all in and trying to make sense of it* all. *The titles were familiar.* Moby-Dick. Frankenstein. Alice's Adventures in Wonderland. *The authors were familiar, too. Herman Melville. Mary Shelley. Lewis Carroll. But what had been done with the covers depicting these iconic characters? Was that Frankenstein—in* blackface? *When did Alice become a little Brown girl trekking through Wonderland? Meanwhile, back at the Penguin Random House and Barnes & Noble corporate offices, as if synchronized, cell phones began to ring and email messages flooded inboxes at a furious pace. Miguel, Aleph, and countless others were registering their complaints, their* disbelief, *about the Barnes & Noble "diversity gaffe" of 2020.*

You may have missed it, but on February 5, Penguin Random House and Barnes & Noble Fifth Avenue announced a bold plan to "kick off Black History Month" by giving twelve classic young-adult texts new covers, known as Diverse Editions. The reimagined classics would include *Alice's Adventures in Wonderland, Romeo and Juliet, Dr. Jekyll and Mr. Hyde, Treasure Island, Emma* . . . well, you get the idea. According to Barnes & Noble, "Each title would have five culturally diverse custom covers designed to ensure the recognition, representation, and inclusion of various multiethnic backgrounds reflected across the country. . . . as part of a new initiative to champion diversity in literature." The publisher created the diverse custom covers by darkening the complexions of these iconic literary figures. Imagine, as observed by Miguel and Aleph, *Frankenstein* and *Peter Pan* in blackface.

## WHY THIS IS PROBLEMATIC

In a world where it is rare for monolithic companies like Barnes & Noble to make large, expensive, public statements aimed at highlighting racial disparity and aiming to do better, this campaign seemed to some to be a positive step. It seemed bold. Artists had been hired, money had been invested, and timelines had been met. However, the campaign went only skin deep, covering up the broader issue, if you will. Essentially, Barnes & Noble could see and partially address only one of the issues: kids of color did not see themselves in much of popular literature, on book covers, in illustrations. They aimed to correct that by making the covers reflect racial diversity. The problem was, Alice was still white, and so were all of the authors most frequently celebrated.

We know that as long as the publishing industry has existed in the United States it has underrepresented most rising identities. Not only are the authors published largely white, so too are their characters, narratives, and messages. This lack of diversity is not a surprise, as a study by Lee & Low Books in 2015 showed that 79 percent of the industry is white, 78 percent female, 88 percent straight, and 92 percent nondisabled.[1] Lacking diversity across all identities limits the ability of people with rising identities to find themselves in stories, connect and empathize with characters, and be inspired by them.

The public backlash was swift and fierce, producing more than two thousand comments in twenty-four hours. Recurring themes among the comments included but were not limited to these: "Why not just promote diverse authors?" "Blackface is racist." "These stories are not representative of the African American nor other people of color's experience." And several versions of "Who actually signed off on such a bad idea?"

Notably, in the mid-pandemic, transnational Black Lives Matter movement and the post–George Floyd era, we witnessed hundreds of corporations pressed into making changes. In efforts to communicate diverse, inclusive values, websites and storefronts alike posted notices and banners that read something like, "We're Listening. We're Learning. We're Acting." Only time will tell how many of these banners are accompanied by sustainable change that moves corporate America through and beyond diversity to actual inclusivity. Making a visual statement could impact people for a moment, and might increase your sales (we worry the proliferation of these statements might solely be motivated by sales), but will not catalyze the long-term change we are hungry for.

### WHAT TO DO ABOUT IT—AS AN ORGANIZATION

Thanks to public comments, Barnes & Noble quickly recognized its error. The company issued a statement that read:

We acknowledge the voices who have expressed concern about the Diverse Editions project at our Fifth Avenue store and have decided to suspend the initiative. Diverse Editions presented new covers of classic books through a series of limited-edition jackets, designed by artists hailing from different ethnicities and backgrounds. The covers are no substitute for black voices or writers of color, whose work and voices deserve to be heard. The booksellers who championed this initiative did so convinced it would help drive engagement with these classic titles. It was a project inspired by our work with schools and was created in part to raise awareness and discussion during Black History Month, in which Barnes & Noble stores nationally will continue to highlight a wide selection of books to celebrate black history and great literature from writers of color.[2]

There are many strengths in the company's response, as it named the problematic nature of the project (that it could appear to be a substitute for Black voices) and committed to taking future actions (lifting up Black voices when celebrating Black History Month). While it may feel awkward and uncomfortable for corporations to admit such errors in judgment, we believe there are additional steps they can take to elevate these public responses to the next level.

As with the Barnes & Noble diversity gaffe, we will all make multiple missteps when taking steps to become more inclusive. For any organization moving toward making change, there won't be, nor should there be, a universal corrective response. However, we propose a four-step framework based in behavioral health clinical practice, illustrated here by asking, "What might Barnes & Noble have done next?"

*Retract.* Apologize quickly and nondefensively, taking ownership. Barnes & Noble did so when it swiftly withdrew the campaign. The retraction noted, "The booksellers who championed this initiative did so convinced it would help drive engagement with these classic titles." Like all apologies in this domain, there is room for growth and expansion. For example, they could have first acknowledged the failure to truly value Black History Month. Black History Month should be more than a new sales campaign. It should mean not only promoting Black authors during the month of February, but committing to efforts to elevate Black voices and experiences through literature on a year-round basis.

Sometimes we forget a simple truth: that corporate decisions and choices are made by individuals. A natural, human urge that most of us have when we mess up is to make the feelings of embarrassment, shame, or guilt "go away." Consequently, we try to apologize too quickly. The retraction may be the most important of the four-step process. As embarrassing and challenging as this may be for corporations, and specifically for the individuals who made the mistakes, an authentic retraction that demonstrates a full understanding of the blunder will engage and hold the attention of the recipient. Anything less will sound lackluster and, likely, will further alienate those you have offended. If this happens, steps 2–4 have absolutely no shot of being realized. So take a moment to "sleep on it." Imagine how Miguel and Aleph might have responded to this alternate example: "We recognize that our actions did not acknowledge or correct the enduring problem of failing to promote and amplify Black authors, voices, and experiences. The use of 'blackface' and erasure was insensitive and hurtful." This type of fully voiced apology can be challenging, as it requires leadership to take complete ownership of the mistake as opposed to passing some of the blame to the "booksellers" or the "artists hailing from different ethnicities and backgrounds."

*Reflect.* It is crucial that Barnes & Noble takes time to understand how this mistake was born. The answer typically is lack of diversity in key decision-making roles within the organization, also known as white dominance. A longstanding history of white CEOs and leaders, who are not forced to think about race on a daily basis, will always be reflected in how organizations interface with consumers and the communities they ostensibly serve. Clearly, Barnes & Noble is not an outlier but rather reflects the national statistics. Only three Fortune

500 CEOs are Black, and yes, all three are men. According to labor force statistics, only 8 percent of managers and 3.8 percent of CEOs are Black. Reflecting on issues of inclusiveness is hard because it requires introspection and an anti-racist stance. It requires acknowledging that a likely majority-white leadership was not able to anticipate how this campaign could be so hurtful. It requires acknowledging how accustomed we are to the dominance of white voices, and of white authors writing what we come to understand as "normal" and universally true. It requires acknowledging that white voices do not and cannot speak for more than 50 percent of the populace. Specific to hiring and retention, it means acknowledging the research that résumés submitted with "white-sounding" names are more likely to lead to interviews compared to résumés submitted with names that are associated with African American or Asian American ethnicity—*even when a company promotes itself as "pro-diversity."* It means looking at company statistics on hiring and retention rates of employees of color compared to white employees and examining who is hired, at what levels of the organization, how long they remain with the company, and who gets promoted.

*Retrain.* While we may know the answers, the ways that whiteness permeates each company specifically must be addressed. This would be an excellent time to hire an external diversity and inclusion expert. This is not the time to ask the people of color at the company to explain why this went wrong, how it happened, and what should be done about it. A painful start to Black History Month is not the time to heap the emotional burden of explaining and teaching onto staff of color who are fatigued from a lifetime of managing these issues. To be clear, there's never a good time for that. Mary-Frances Winters, author of *Black Fatigue: How Racism Erodes the Mind, Body, and Spirit*, wrote,

> Black people have been marching, protesting, resisting, writing, orating, praying, legislating, and commentating for centuries for equity and justice, and—young and old—we are fatigued. It is physically, mentally, and emotionally draining to continue to experience inequities and even atrocities day after day when justice,

equity, and fairness are purportedly legislated rights of all citizens in America.[3]

Take a lesson from the *American Dirt* dustup, which reignited controversy about cultural appropriation and, according to writer Roxane Gay, "about who gets to write about the lives of people of color and how they are compensated."[4] *American Dirt* author Jeanine Cummins, who identifies as white, received a seven-figure advance for the novel about Mexican migrants fleeing drug cartels. As publishing and other industries strive to become more diverse, ensure that a full range of diverse voices are at the corporate table. Once your employees have received in-depth training to increase their cultural awareness and humility, increase the diversity across a range of sociocultural identities of your workforce. Create channels for people with rising identities to advance through your company. Acknowledge that working while Black within a largely white institution is laborious and comes with a heavy and cumulative dose of burnout occurring on a daily, weekly, and yearly basis. Meet this higher burden with financial and promotional acknowledgment.

*Re-approach.* The opportunity to re-approach is a gift that, once earned, must be valued. For Barnes & Noble, it means making an informed and sustained attempt to address the issue it originally sought to highlight. The company has a significant platform that could elevate and amplify the countless talented Black, Indigenous, and People of Color (BIPOC) authors who have been waiting far too long to be recognized. What if Barnes & Noble used its platform to feature these underrepresented authors year-round? Teachers such as Miguel and Aleph would have an embarrassment of riches from which to formulate lesson plans and engage their students. If even a small fraction of their seventh- and eighth-graders felt inspired to stick with literature and creative writing, the opportunity to "re-approach" would be the gift that keeps on giving.

The banners we referenced earlier in this chapter that read "We're Listening. We're Learning. We're Acting." were from the apparel and gifts corporation Anthropologie. In mid-2020, Instagram lit up with allegations that Anthropologie engaged in racial profiling (including using code words for Black shoppers), hired predominantly white employees, and "whitewashed" or culturally appropriated products. Model and influencer Lydia Okello reported on Instagram that the company asked them to work on a Pride Month campaign without compensation. Here's a bit of what we found beneath the Anthropologie banner. As you review the substance of the company's response, do you see evidence of the four-step Re-tract, Reflect, Retrain, and Re-approach framework?

Our Promise to Our Community
UPDATED June 19th, 2020:

Anthropologie was founded on the values and principles of inclusiveness and cultural understanding. Every day, we strive to do better, to be better—to better serve our customers and our community.

Discriminatory behavior or bias, in any and every form and expression, has no place at Anthropologie. We reject racism. We stand with the Black community and believe that Black lives matter. We are deeply saddened and disturbed by reports of racial profiling in our stores, and we apologize, profusely and unequivocally, to any customer who was made to feel unwelcome.

As a company, we are making impactful changes that address our commitment to the Black community. We are taking the following actions:

- We have hired an external third party to conduct a comprehensive review of our store practices. We have a zero-tolerance policy regarding discrimination or racial profiling in any form.
- We formed an internal, cross-functional Diversity & Inclusivity (D&I) Committee to develop an actionable strategy in partnership with our Executive Team (including Shared Services) and outside consultants.

- We will conduct mandatory D&I training for all store employees to be completed by July 30th. All Home Office teams will participate in similar training.
- We will expand our recruiting efforts at Historically Black Colleges and Universities.
- We will increase representation of Black models, influencers, and brand partners.

We are making these additional commitments:

- We are sponsoring a full four-year scholarship for a young Black student pursuing studies in fashion design. We hope that the first scholarship will be awarded to an individual for the upcoming academic year. As a global fashion retailer, we embrace our position to empower the next generation of aspiring Black artists, designers, and creators. It is our duty to do so.
- We will help rebuild and grow businesses in Black communities.
- We are making a donation of $100,000 to the United Negro College Fund. We are making a 3:1 employee donation match to this organization and to contributions made to:
  - The Innocence Project
  - The Antiracist Research and Policy Center
  - The Equal Justice Initiative
  - Year Up[5]

At this time, perhaps more than ever, there will be a groundswell of cases across industries we can learn from in order to practice and implement new strategies for correcting instances of good ideas gone bad. The Barnes & Noble incident won't be the last attempt to "promote diversity" that misses the mark. Toni Morrison poignantly said, "Definitions belong to the definers, not to the defined."[3] In other words, the most effective, authentic, and sincere way of promoting diversity is to have diverse decision-makers and authors sitting at the boardroom table and in critical leadership positions throughout the industry. When this happens, the concepts that were patently obvious to many people of color and to the hundreds of white people who felt compelled to post their dissenting comments in this case will become intuitive. Strategies such as promoting Black writers or featuring classics about diverse experiences will be free-flowing and plentiful.

### WHAT TO DO ABOUT IT—AS AN INDIVIDUAL

There is work to be done on an individual level as well. While we do not know, we can imagine that there might have been an employee at Barnes & Noble, let's call her Danni, who suggested Diverse Editions in the first place. Even a committee-generated idea had to have originated with an employee. For the sake of sharing our model of how to respond when you've messed up, we will imagine Danni is white. She wanted to do the right thing and identified as holding social justice values. When the bad news broke and the world responded, there is no doubt that Danni felt crestfallen. She likely felt embarrassed and attempted to lay low at her desk, dreading every approaching footstep. *Please don't let those footsteps mean someone is coming to talk to me.* We like to imagine that Danni eventually (would have or perhaps quickly) absorbed the embarrassment, composed herself, and addressed the situation. Below are guidelines one can reference when recovering from a personal blunder.

*Acknowledge.* Even if you don't know quite what to say, acknowledging that something bad happened/is happening is a powerful first step. If a coworker were to approach Danni to share that there was a stream of comments on the Internet, Danni might say, "Wow, I didn't see that coming, and I am going to need some time to take it in." She might nod when hearing the news while taking a deep breath, and then simply say, "Okay, I am glad I know this now."

*Take time.* Pause to process on your own and with people who share your privileged identities. It is totally appropriate for Danni to ask for the rest of the day off to reflect. This way she can sigh, lament, and cry in private. Taking this time to process on her own reduces the burden on her colleagues of color. She can express her surprise and confusion. She can call white friends and vent. She could work through her defensiveness with her white friends and brainstorm with them about why her idea was wrong, and how it happened in the first place. She can go online and search for articles on the lack of racial diversity in her industry and read proposed causes and solutions. She can read firsthand accounts of those who differ from her to better understand their experiences without having to ask the one Black woman in the office to explain why the campaign was a problem.

*Apologize.* Either while Danni is away or when she returns to work, she could send a brief email to her team or those who expressed hurt. She might say, "I want to acknowledge that my idea was hurtful to many people. The campaign was understandably experienced as an attempt at erasure of Black voices and/or glossing over huge problems within the publishing world—racism and a lack of diversity. I am committed to being a part of any efforts made in response to this and to joining with colleagues as we identify and implement strategies to make positive change in our industry and the literature we offer our readers. I will continue to reflect on this experience, and welcome any conversations that people would like to have." You will notice many levels of acknowledgement and action in this example. First, the apology acknowledged and validated the emotions and experiences of people of color in response to the campaign. Second, the history of the lack of diversity in the publishing world was clearly named as problematic for the company and the industry as a whole. Third, commitments to changing both internally (via self-reflection and education) and externally (systemic change) were stated. We will go through these steps in more detail in the following chapter.

*Motivate change.* Going forward, Danni could use her new learning to lobby for change within her company. She might speak to her manager or someone else in leadership, highlighting the lack of racial diversity in the company and the need for increased representation. She could share statistics that show that teams rich in sociocultural identities are more creative and have better productivity. Further, she might team up with others engaging in this work to communicate the need for increased racial diversity at all levels of the organization. A statement might include motivators such as "This is where companies are headed. Soon it will be embarrassing to have such a white workforce. Don't you want to be ahead of that wave? As an industry leader we should set the model for others to follow . . . and the good press wouldn't hurt either."

Of course, not all mistakes occur on such a large scale as this. In fact, some of our most important and impactful work will be done in identifying when we have engaged in or observed brief identity-related aggressions and knowing how to respond effectively in the moment. These are often one-on-one, personal interactions where we act from implicit bias. See chapter 10 about navigating these types of mistakes.

*Seek inspiration.* Whether recovering from missteps as an organization or on an individual level, it can help to be inspired. The competitive drive to succeed in the marketplace can override the process of noting and learning from progressive actions others are taking across industries. While many companies are reticent to take a stand on social justice issues for fear of being perceived as making political statements (note: the Black Lives Matter movement and gay rights are social issues that are often politicized), many have taken bold leaps. Those maneuvers can even pay off and improve the company's standing in the minds of many of their customers.

For example, much has been written and debated about Nike's bold and, many thought at the time, controversial decision to feature Colin Kaepernick as a face of its iconic "Just Do It" campaign in 2018. Kaepernick is the former starting quarterback for the San Francisco 49ers who, by taking a knee during the playing of the national anthem to protest police brutality and injustice, inspired a movement. As a result, he has not worked in the NFL since. The Nike/"Just Do It"/Colin Kaepernick story will undoubtedly provide substantive fodder for business school case studies and journals for years to come. The ad read simply, "Believe in something. Even if it means sacrificing everything." Despite having never been employed again by the NFL, Kaepernick's social justice activism has garnered him international recognition, including the Harvard W. E. B. Du Bois Medal, *Sports Illustrated*'s Muhammad Ali Legacy Award, the Amnesty International Ambassador of Consciousness Award, and many others. The former NFL quarterback's jersey sales have skyrocketed since he took that fateful knee, and he has committed to channeling the proceeds back into the community.[6]

For Barnes & Noble, Anthropologie, Nike, and other corporations, the real inspiration will come when we see evidence of their statements, banners, and campaigns reflected in the quality of life enjoyed by their most marginalized and underrepresented employees. As Darren Walker, president of the Ford Foundation, noted during the protests over police killings of Black people in 2020, "Corporate America can no longer get away with token responses to systemic problems. It is going to take a systemic response to sufficiently address this crisis that has been decades in the making."[7] Noting that "Justice is not a trend and corporate statements and murals are not enough," nonprofit organizations such as Beyond the Statement have emerged to ensure that "corporations affirm their support for Black lives" by taking actions that improve workplace conditions and the quality of peoples' lives.[8] Reading about stories like these and saving them in a "feel inspired" folder on your desktop, or printing a picture for your office to serve as a reminder, can help you maintain inspiration and motivation to do this important work.

# CHAPTER 8

# LEADING BY EMPOWERING LISTENING

· Justin's Story ·

*In late spring 2020, Justin, a white, cisgender, male CEO of an invest-ment firm, was settling into the new protocols and routines instituted during the novel coronavirus pandemic. After an initial jolt, the finan-cial markets were beginning to stabilize even after millions of workers had lost their jobs when the economy came to a screeching halt. Record numbers of people were filing for weekly unemployment benefits, with no end in sight. The disease was on the ebb on the East Coast, where weeks earlier the daily body counts had totaled in the thousands, but was just beginning to leave its mark across the nation. At Justin's firm, which had a worldwide workforce, there had been minimal spread of the virus. Most workers were privileged to continue working, but from the relative safety of home or even a second home. Then on June 1, Justin woke to news that would shift the conversation away from the virus—at his firm, across the nation, and around the globe—and in novel and unexpected ways.*

*Every morning news show, even the especially sunny and chatty ones, was rebroadcasting video of life slowly and inexorably being taken from George Floyd, an unarmed Black man who was killed when a Minneap-olis police officer knelt on his neck for more than nine minutes during an arrest. It was disturbing to watch, but Justin, like the rest of the world, could not bring himself to turn away from it. This must be what his best friend, a seasoned news editor, referred to as "a story with legs," Justin thought. As he sipped his coffee, he opened his email and saw an emerging trend, something all successful market-watching investors learn to do early in their careers. Still, he hadn't seen this one coming. The pace became exponential, emails flooding in like an avalanche; he'd never seen anything like it. He began to open them, one after the other. They were letters of acknowledgment from different corporations, organizations, and even small local businesses he frequented. There they sat among his email messages, as if mocking his ineptitude. They were poignant letters openly acknowledging the growing feelings of loss, anger, and frustration, spreading like a virus, following the killing of George Floyd. As the leader of the firm, Justin wondered if he should issue a similar statement. Should he somehow address the trauma that his employees of color were likely enduring? He stared into his cereal bowl and wondered, Would it be awkward if I sent a message now? What would I even say? Why hadn't the communications department reached out to propose something? Paralysis set in as the anxiety of not knowing what to do soared. He hit "refresh," and the thoughtfully crafted messages from others kept coming. It became clear that this trend was all encompassing. In coming days, Justin looked on as the corporate emails mounted and soon morphed into detailed plans of antiracist actions being taken. Funds were being allocated. Policies were being examined for bias. Board members were resigning to make room for people of color. He couldn't explain it, nor could he comprehend why this time seemed different from countless others, but something had shifted. His feelings of embarrassment gave way to dread and sometimes shame. Why hadn't he thought of drafting something sooner? He wondered, Is it already too late? Did I miss the moment? How will I catch up when I don't even know where to begin?*

*Justin picked up the phone and called André, a trusted colleague. He thought of André because he's Black. "André, can you even believe this? What should we do?!" André sighed; the line filled with silence.*

## THE TIDE TURNS

George Floyd's murder catalyzed new levels of awareness and change. Like a visual oxymoron, Black Lives Matter signs adorned suburban lawns where redlining and housing discrimination had always been the thoughtless practice. The beautiful, bright-yellow murals snaked like a refurbished locomotive lurching from Sixteenth Street NW in DC all the way to Allston Way in Berkeley, California. Book clubs were launched by white neighbors and friends eager to learn about white privilege. Titles once viewed as provocative, like *How to Be an Antiracist* and *White Fragility*, were now seen as essential and were flying off bookstore shelves (if the stores were actually open) and on back order. Marcus Books, the oldest Black-owned bookstore in America, was enjoying an unprecedented boom in business as faithful and new customers sought knowledge, solace, and fellowship in the Oakland institution. People of color watched as many of their white colleagues started processing the pain and racism within our country for the very first time. No longer was it sufficient to merely celebrate Black History Month. During the summer of 2020 in America, anti-racism became *the* big thing. Declarations that Black lives matter were in vogue, and white leadership had no idea what to do. Like Justin, people around the world woke up on June 1 wanting to do *something*, change *something*, and examine the ways in which they or their organizations and institutions were scaffolding structural racism.

George Floyd's murder seemed to anoint white people who never really had to see or think about race with a kind of 2020 vision. And what did organizations do next? Leadership all over the globe turned to the people of color in their industries and asked, "What should we do differently?" Of course, in the grand scheme of things, this seismic culture shift and the urgent desire to ignite change were significant and positive occurrences. However, it must be acknowledged that for years, people with rising identities have been speaking up within institutions and calling out the need for change. And for just as long, their voices have been ignored or silenced.

By Wednesday of the following week that June, ABC had announced the first Black bachelor on its iconic franchise *The Bachelor*. Organizations pledged to move large amounts of money toward diversity and inclusion efforts, without a plan. Even popular dating sites offered users the chance to display Black Lives Matter badges on their profiles. It was fascinating for us (the authors) to see how money and infrastructure could be moved in mere hours once people decided to care—or knew it would hurt their brand if they appeared not to care. For decades leadership in many organizations simply claimed, "We'd do it if we had the funds," when it came to addressing diversity, equity, and inclusion in their offices. But now, as organizational trainers on intersectionality and inclusivity, our phones were ringing off the hook and emails clamoring for training were pouring in. Although we were eager to meet the moment and the demand, like so many others, we felt a rush of conflicting emotions. There was something confusing and maddening about being asked to instruct an institution on how to change when so many voices had long been silenced on these issues or treated with indifference. Why did it take another death for organizations to begin to look inward and begin to see the corrosive effects of inaction and indifference? How come all of the other Black lives didn't matter enough?

## WHY THIS IS A PROBLEM

Once the United States finally woke up, institutional leaders—whether motivated by genuine insight, risk of losing reputation, or both—knew they needed to commit to change. They kept asking and asking, "What should we do now?" Unfortunately, this incessant asking came after a very long period of not listening. Thus, Black individuals within institutions everywhere were not only dealing with the personal trauma and international unrest brought about by George Floyd's killing; they were exhausted from being ignored, silenced, and/or under-resourced (whether financially, in administrative support, or in public encouragement by leadership) throughout their tenure at these same organizations. At the same time, some BIPOC employees were being heavily relied upon to carry the increased emotional labor of instructing their institutions.

In business terms, this was a poorly managed investment. Employees of color, gender-queer employees, Indigenous employees, and employees with disabilities offer unique experiential insight on how to make your business better. If leadership had been listening all along, they would not have needed to ask what to do, and they would have known that this moment of racialized trauma was not the right moment to ask. If leadership had been listening, they would have known not to ask the folks being marginalized to do the work to fix the very organization that had been marginalizing them. If leadership doesn't listen, they forfeit the opportunity to learn.

Of course this wasn't only a phenomenon of the George Floyd era. The cycle of ignoring, silencing, and asking occurs across identities and institutions on a daily basis. Take a look at the following examples to see if you recognize any trends:

QUEER EMPLOYEE: "I'm sad that I've never been able to vacation in a warm place in the world where I am totally comfortable holding my partner's hand. When I share this with people, I always get a list of recommendations, which I appreciate. But when I go excitedly Googling the list I still find stats of hate crimes and recommendations against showing signs of affection in public. In some ways that hurts even more."

STRAIGHT BOSS: "Oh, you know, I really would highly recommend Tel Aviv. It's highly diverse and I think you and your wife would be so comfortable there!"

EMPLOYEE WITH A PHYSICAL DISABILITY: "It seems like the parking spots designated for people with disabilities are always full by the time I arrive at 8 a.m."

ABLE-BODIED SUPERVISOR: "Yeah, the parking situation here really sucks. There are times when I have to park so far away that the walk from the lot to my office adds another fifteen minutes to my commute!"

GAY EMPLOYEE: "Coming out was really hard and caused a lot of tension in my family for years."

STRAIGHT EMPLOYEE: "I'm so glad it's way better now than it would have been thirty years ago!"

BLACK EMPLOYEE: "As an employee of color who is working to advance here, it's discouraging to see that Kimberly, who is of African heritage, has stayed in the same position in the company for five years, while Amanda, who is white, has been promoted twice in less time."

WHITE SUPERVISOR: "They are totally different people. I don't think Kimberly even wants a promotion. She seems really happy with her role."

FEMALE EMPLOYEE: "When I participated on that national panel last week, they introduced all of the male panelists by their titles and called me by my first name. It felt weird."

MALE EMPLOYEE: "At least you were invited. That was a huge deal and will look great on your résumé. You did a great job, too."

If you are anything like us, you felt physical discomfort just reading these examples. These are real interactions collected throughout our interviews, and they happen multiple times every day. We coined the terms "Oppressive Listening" and "Empowering Listening" to highlight harmful and helpful listening behaviors within identity-related discussions.

Oppressive Listening, portrayed in the examples above, skips empathy and validation. There is no pause for the Listener to imagine what emotions the Speaker might have felt and might be feeling in the moment. There is no expression of empathy. There is no acknowledgment of the existence of oppression in the world, in the workplace, or in the specific experience shared by the Speaker. Oppressive Listening bypasses all of that and heads directly to problem solving. Oppressive Listening shifts the affect, focus, and/or agenda of the dialogue away from the Speaker and onto the Listener. Suddenly the Listener has the stage while they brainstorm solutions or express their shock and surprise.

It's no coincidence that the Oppressive Listening behavioral style is so common among organizational leaders. Leaders in our society have been groomed to be unemotional, outcome-driven, efficient problem solvers who find the path of least resistance—and these skills are often powerful in creating robust and effective teams.

Historically, leadership positions have been occupied by those with privileged identities: white, male, able-bodied, cisgender, straight or not out. Those same individuals have been socialized to take up space in the room, assert their dominance, and tap their internal resources for the answers to problems.

Having a hierarchical workspace that relies upon this approach may not be as problematic when the organization is comprised of all white cisgender men, as many workspaces once were. However, once identity differences are entered into the mix, the recipe for success changes. As women and people of color started entering workspaces previously dominated by white men, inevitable cross-identity tensions were catalyzed. The same tensions are manifesting now as trans* and gender-queer or gender-neutral individuals are starting to come out in the workplace. Having an employee whose pronouns are they/them introduces a whole new language to the team and a whole new growth edge, often bringing mistakes and consequent pain. When reports of painful, cross-identity interactions (identity-related aggressions, overt racism) surface within an organization, a flurry of actions may be set into motion. These can include, for example, an escalation of Human Resources interventions and the need for increased company education. When these instances are brought to leadership, responding quickly with "fixes" is a time-honored corporate response but not the most effective strategy.

Instead, we encourage leadership to take time and engage in training to build their Empowering Listening skills. Empowering Listening emphasizes giving the Speaker, the historically marginalized colleague in the scenario, the stage for the entire interaction. The Speaker is given the reins and gets to decide whether the dialogue moves to a problem-solving phase. Below, we outline types of Oppressive Listening, how to catch yourself falling into these common traps, and how to increase your Empowering Listening skills. Of course it all starts with trust and a willingness to have the conversation. Empowering Listening is an interactive process that requires the willingness to hear and the trust to disclose experiences that may never have been shared before.

## WHAT TO DO ABOUT IT

As Imani Perry wrote on Twitter, "Every single US industry is about to roil under revelations about the ubiquity of racism. The measure of decency will not be how well they defend against the charges but whether they are willing to listen and act in meaningful ways. Put down the shield, open the windows."[1] These words call for a stance of openness across industries at a time when defensiveness will likely be the default. It will be easier to "put down the shield" if you prepare yourself to hear experiences of race-based trauma.

*Broach the topic.* Dr. Kenneth V. Hardy, a racial trauma therapist, scholar, and president of the Eikenberg Academy for Social Justice, reminds practitioners that in therapeutic settings they are "the brokers of permission" to acknowledge the influence of race on relationships. This is an excellent practice that we encourage organizational leaders who hold privilege across identities to exercise in the workplace when appropriate.

Acknowledge when pertinent events are happening in the media. Make room to check in and see how people are doing at the beginning of staff meetings. Expect that people who hold rising identities might not want to process their feelings on any given issue or event in a room full of people who don't identify like them. Expect that these conversations will be awkward initially. Don't give up.

*Uncouple expertise from leadership.* It's almost reflexive for leaders to lean into the issues and challenges where they hold "expert" status, as we all gravitate toward our respective comfort zones. Effective leadership in the realm of inclusivity can be counterintuitive. Here, leadership requires cultural humility. Cultural humility is an approach and philosophy developed by two female physicians of color, Drs. Melanie Tervalon and Jann Murray-Garcia, in 1998 to create more just and equitable hospital systems and more culturally responsive practitioners in the aftermath of the riots following the Rodney King beating in 1991 and acquittal of the police officers involved in 1992. Cultural humility principles are pertinent to Empowering Listening and include many of the recurring themes in this book. The contrast between the practice of cultural competence and cultural humility is illuminating. The former suggests that understanding another's cultural experiences can be achieved or accomplished as with any other discrete body of knowledge or literature. Check the following boxes and you too can be certified as culturally competent! Cultural humility recognizes that there is no endpoint to learning about another culture. This work requires ongoing critical self-reflection; recognition of and striving to address power imbalances (such as doctor-patient, teacher-student, or supervisor-employee); and highlights the expertise that resides in the community among, in the above examples, patients, students, and staff.

*Listen. Listen. Listen, listen, listen.* This has been a top-tier recommendation for those interacting across differences for decades. If you hold privilege in an aspect of identity, you will never be the expert on the experience of holding marginalization within that identity. You will always be learning and the content will always be changing. We know what you're thinking: "I get it, already. Listen. Will do!" (Love the enthusiasm there!) However, there are ways to listen, ways not to listen, and microevents within conversations that are worth highlighting and unpacking.

*Learn before you listen.* Listening means listening the right way, with the singular goal of understanding the Speaker. Listening does not mean allowing the other person to speak for a turn, then reverting back to being the one doing the talking. Listening does not mean generating the optimal response inside your head while the Speaker is talking. How many times have you heard a well-intentioned person with privilege open a meeting by saying, "I am here to listen," only to spend most of the allotted time speaking? Recently, Lauren was meeting with a multicultural group within an organization. When she and her colleagues arrived at the meeting, they were greeted by board members of the organization, who introduced themselves, stating, "We're here to listen and don't want to take up space." The group was advertised as a space for healing in the wake of George Floyd's murder, but the gathering quickly morphed into a platform for addressing the needs and priorities of the board members. Perhaps you have had a chance to join these types of encounters, which have occurred all across organizations. Those who were invited to heal were asked to offer the board ideas for how the organization could be better. In this specific case, the board members allowed a bit of space for these ideas related to healing to surface, but each time an idea was offered, it was obvious that the board members were itching to respond. They shifted in their seats, lost eye contact with the speakers, and didn't allow other group members to participate and build upon one another's ideas. Whenever there was a pause, they blurted out statements such as "We want more diversity on the board. We don't have much diversity because enough people of color don't apply. We think you should work on getting people of color to apply." In summary, the board members co-opted a space that had been designated for another purpose, elevated their agenda, and proceeded to model Oppressive Listening. They solicited solutions from the marginalized members of the group and then summarily dismissed their contributions with explanations like "We can't do that because our organization isn't structured that way" (a great example of how these oppressive systems have been maintained over centuries). As the same old dynamic was unfolding, the board was oblivious to the pattern of institutionalized oppression it was reenacting. In times of crisis, leadership turns to the most marginalized folks within an organization, invites their participation and wisdom, and then silences them. This dangerous and stifling cycle happens over and over and must be disrupted because leadership that is defensive, silencing, and marginalizing is experienced as ineffective, disheartening, and demoralizing.

How could board members have listened better? They could have stuck to their stated goal of not taking up space. They could have listened actively to suggestions, by nodding, maintaining eye contact with speakers, leaning forward, and taking notes. They could have expressed their gratitude by saying, "Thank you for taking the time to educate us and for sharing these creative suggestions with us." They could have communicated their commitment to future actions including taking the ideas back to the full board. They could have acknowledged and validated the palpable pain and distress in the room and resisted the urge to leap to immediate problem solving. Below are additional strategies for building your Empowering Listening skills and for catching Oppressive Listening traps.

## RESIST OPPRESSIVE LISTENING

*Suppress your surprise.* Responding to an Indigenous colleague's story of being marginalized in a group meeting with "WHAT!? I can't believe that happened! I can't believe anyone would ever do something like that! I don't know how you put up with that!" is not helpful. Enthusiastically expressing your surprise (and therefore naivete) about experiences of marginalization takes the emotional stage. Suddenly you're the one with big emotions, which enlists your colleague of Indigenous heritage to bring you back to baseline by explaining, educating, and, as is often the case, comforting. This behavior underscores how you've been able to go through life without needing to think about others' oppression (at least in that one domain). This behavior reminds your colleague, who has already communicated their personal distress and hurt, about how little you've considered the ways in which their identity has been structurally and historically marginalized and how that undoubtedly has played out at work. This behavior demonstrates your lack of appreciation for how hard they have had to work, absorb, accept, and repress in order to get to work and to perform. Sharing your surprise and asking, "How is that even possible?!" is like plopping the moldy cherry on top of the sour ice cream sundae that no one wants any part of. Instead, offer validating nonverbals such as a head shake, a nod, a gentle sigh, or an empathetic facial expression. Offer thanks and recognition: "As a white, nonindigenous person, I had not thought about that before and I can totally see how that could happen. That is not okay. I (the person you trusted enough to confide in) and we (the organization) will do better."

*Check your emotions.* This might sound odd coming from two psychologists. We'll clarify. This is not a recommendation to ignore or suppress what you (the Listener) feel when a colleague discloses an incident of bias or racism. As is true for many Black, Indigenous, and People of Color (BIPOC) who are in leadership positions, trainees, students, and colleagues have sought me (Stephanie) out to disclose and process all categories of bias incidents. I won't lie: holding and receiving these narratives, while also checking my own emotions, gets more challenging with every occurrence. I am grateful and humbled that people trust me enough to share events that can be confusing, distressing, and even paralyzing. Sometimes I have the strongest urge to cry. Sometimes I do cry. Still, I remain mindful to check my emotions because I do want the focus to remain on the Speaker. Most important, I want my colleague or trainee to feel free to share what needs to be shared in that moment. To cry or not to cry can be a tricky question and there isn't a one-size-fits-all approach here. Crying can be a vulnerable and powerful way of demonstrating empathy. At the same time, it can risk shutting down the dialogue because your colleague or trainee feels compelled to take care of your distress or at least not burden you further. Fortunately, I have others at work and at home on whom I can rely for emotional support. We recommend using your emotions to inform what future actions to take. If, for example, I didn't channel my sadness into constructive actions, I would not have the capacity to continue to absorb these narratives. It simply would not be sustainable. We recommend building and relying upon your own support network for processing your own feelings. (See chapter 3, the Multicultural Psychology Peer Consultation team for discussion of one workplace model.)

*Avoid comparisons and analogies.* As humans, we default to looking for ways we relate to people within interactions. It is very typical when hearing a friend share how hard it is to be the only Muslim employee in the office, surrounded by Christmas and Hanukkah decorations, to respond with "Ugh, I *totally* get it! It's so rough being the only trans* person in the office." Of course, both experiences are valid and deserve time and space for processing. However, jumping right in with your experience shifts the focus, signals to the other person that this is not solely their time to process, and communicates that you think you both share the same experience, which is impossible. Instead, note that you feel comfortable sharing with them what it's like to be the only trans* person in the workplace, and pin it for a later date. Acknowledge that you cannot imagine what that would feel like, and that you imagine it feels isolating, frustrating, and maybe lonely.

*Avoid fixing.* As a cisgender white person, I (Lauren), was socialized to take up space in conversations, was taught that I am inherently smart, and will naturally come up with good solutions to problems. I was taught to fix problems that present themselves. I was taught (likely linked to my European American ethnicity) that emotions just get in the way. So when people share their pain related to identities, my knee-jerk reaction is to attempt to "fix" the situation. Instead, I need to work to sit with and acknowledge pain, accept that the emotions being expressed are real and valid, and resist jumping to problem solving.

As a straight, cisgender, Christian, able-bodied senior manager with an elite educational background, I (Stephanie) am more likely to miss the privileges associated with these aspects of my identity. These factors intersect with my experiences of being a Black woman in America in complex ways and definitely influence my problem-solving strategies. With age and experience, I have grown less patient and more intolerant of identity-related aggressions in the workplace. I am more likely to take action to address injustices and to seek ways to support others in doing the same, forgetting that junior colleagues and trainees hold less power and authority. Fixing urges come in a number of forms and are driven by positionality.

*There is the "intention" fix.* One might have the urge to respond to a shared identity-related aggression with "Well, I'm sure that isn't what the person *meant*." For example, imagine Tina, a barista who has worked with complicated espresso machines for more than a decade. Her male customer Bill might walk in, see her using tools to repair the machine, and say, "Looks like you might need some help there! Have you even used a tool before?" undermining her specialist training and experience. Tina might share the experience with a colleague, expressing frustration. Her colleague might engage in mental backflips to make sense of why Bill would make those comments, and attempt to explain that rationalization to "remove" Tina's frustration. For example, the colleague might say, "I'm sure he was just trying to help. I think his job involves engineering." The urge to reinterpret and explain intent must be avoided. After all, it is the *impact* of statements that matters most, not the *intent*. Instead, focus on validating the pain: "I am really sorry that happened. That is not okay." Or listen and nod, offering a sigh or a phrase like "Ugh, I'm guessing that's happened before" if you don't know what else to say. No need to fix it at that moment. Just listen.

*There is the "at least" fix.* When we bear witness to or hear about others' experiences of marginalization, it's painful. Certainly, it's only a sliver of what the targeted person holds on a daily basis, but it is painful nonetheless. What do we, as humans, do when we experience uncomfortable emotions? We might try to stop them, escape them, change them, or squash them. Saying "at least it's better now" is an attempt to turn our minds away from the pain—thoughts and images of family rejection based on sexual orientation or gender identity; homeless trans* teens—and toward positive thoughts, such as images of pride parades and gay marriages. Who wouldn't choose to focus on the hopeful and progressive images rather than the rejecting and oppressive ones? This urge is natural and we need to build awareness of these tendencies and work to resist acting on them. Instead, do your duty as an ally and let the pain in. Build your own capacity to feel it and hold it, even if only for a few minutes. There is absolutely no need to sweep the pain away. Rather, feeling the other person's emotional distress (showing empathy) is the greatest gift you can offer. Empathy is the sister to effective systemic transformation.

Relatedly, when people share their identity-related experiences with you, they might be very sad and despondent; they might seem numb; they might be rageful and angry; they might speak in a loud tone, pacing and gesturing. As the Listener it is your job to sit with the big emotions that understandably come up. Allow the person to be angry, and say things such as "You seem angry, and that makes total sense. I am angry just hearing this and I have not had to live it. It is okay to be angry here with me. Anger is such an important emotion that signals that things aren't okay—and they definitely aren't." Offering this type of validation can be especially helpful when big emotions are present. Notice that your body will likely react with fear or anxiety in the presence of anger. Remind yourself that you are not in danger and take deep breaths while you listen.

*There is the action/savior fix.* Responding to your friend's comment with anger, outrage, and surprise, and jumping immediately to "We have to do something about this!" is what we refer to as the action/savior fix. Right there, in that moment, you have taken ownership away from the individual. You've shifted the focus away from their pain to your new mission. You have reinstated the power dynamic of your privilege. Through your actions, however well intended, you've decided that their experience was yours for the taking. Now you own it. When the savior fix transaction takes place, your colleague may or may not feel the desire to speak up in the moment. They might go along with your efforts or just become quiet. Please keep in mind that this fix is a special kind of dangerous. The savior fixer often feels gratified and accomplished but can never shield their friend from possible retaliation. You as a well-intentioned white/straight/cis person might barge into the boss's office declaring the injustice on your friend's behalf. There, your job is done. Your friend, however, may find themselves painted as "too sensitive about gender stuff" or as "an angry black woman." More likely, these perceptions will be expressed as "She's not a team player" or "She doesn't share our collaborative style." Without your or her knowledge, your friend's name may very well be relegated to the bottom of the company's list of rising leaders.

While in some cases "fixing" will lead to positive change, jumping there too fast can be dangerous. Often when we spring into action to address one situation we check it off our list and move on, missing the chance to see the situation within a broader problematic system that needs to be addressed. For example, I (Lauren) noticed that immediately following George Floyd's killing, I was actively seeking out and attending protests, meetings, and related actions. Now, a few months later, I have not attended a protest in several weeks. As humans, we tend to want to take action when we know something bad is happening and everyone is talking about and working on the issue. But we have notoriously short attention spans. Resist the urge to "fix" identity-related issues by hyper-focusing on the event. Extending the timeline of your commitment will draw your attention to the broader context, which might inspire strategies for addressing the systemic issues that made it possible for the event to happen in the first place. So while it certainly was important that I attended protests, I also need to pair those short-term actions with longer-term efforts, such as writing this book or organizing a yearlong series of discussions on race across BIPOC and white people in my small town.

This might feel like a lot. You may be thinking, "It seems like no matter what I do I'm bound to mess up." First, let's just state that you *are* going to mess up. We mess up often. It's not going to be pretty, especially at first, but you *will* get better over time. You will start to feel excited by the work and feel the rewards of your learning as you cultivate relationships with people who have vastly different backgrounds and life experiences from your own. You will feel rewarded knowing that each step you take is reducing the pain and suffering of those you know and those you may never meet. If you hold stock in the business case for sustaining inclusive organizations, you'll reap tangible benefits there, too, as your company's committees, task forces, and boards are transformed into actual teams.

## PRACTICE EMPOWERING LISTENING

*If not fixing, then what?* When delivering Leading by Empowering Listening training to organizations, we field lots of questions about resisting the rush to fix. Indeed, it's counterintuitive. You might be wondering, "If someone tells me about an issue they had, am I supposed to do something about it or not?" As referenced in chapter 3, this work can feel a lot like dancing. Learning the pacing of listening (quietly, with nonverbals), validating ("It's not okay that that happened"), and following the lead of the person in pain informs and guides how quickly or slowly to move toward action planning. This pacing takes time to learn and the dance will vary from partner to partner. As your emotional intelligence increases with practice, you will start to feel the unique pacing within your relationships and across settings. The short answer is, yes, of course there is a time and place for action, but it isn't necessarily your call to make or your place to take the lead. When it is your time to say something (after giving the Speaker center stage), use the following summary of Empowering Listening strategies and practice along with the examples that follow.

*Pause and feel.* After the Speaker has shared their thoughts and story, pause. Take a deep breath and check in with your emotions. Notice what is coming up for you by asking yourself, "Do I feel anger, sadness, defensiveness, surprise?" Breathe through those emotions and allow them to settle. It's fine to be transparent about your need for time. Try saying, "Thank you for sharing that with me. I need a moment to process what I just heard."

*Find empathy.* Imagine what the other person may have felt when the event(s) happened and what they might be feeling now in recounting, and perhaps, re-experiencing, the situation. Validate that they are hurting or have been hurt. Express that their being hurt due to their identities is not okay.

*Name "isms" at all levels.* A key part of Empowering Listening is to name the "ism" at hand, such as racism, ageism, or sexism. If you are a visual learner, try picturing three color-coded, embedded circles. The smallest circle is green and located at the center of the diagram. The Individual (Speaker) and the incident being shared in the moment sit there. The center, green circle requires your immediate attention. The strongest affect (emotion) resides there. The green circle is nested inside a slightly larger yellow circle, which represents your Organization. All of the conditions, structures, policies, and practices that permit and perpetuate oppression in your company are located in the yellow circle. To convey your understanding of the situation most effectively, the "isms" at these levels also should be named, along with a commitment to addressing them. Those two circles are nested within the largest circle, which is red and represents the larger Society. The red circle contains the broader culture, economy, politics, and beliefs of your region or country. Every identity-related incident has Individual/Organizational/Societal influencers and implications. When you are naming and validating the "isms" that you hear in someone's story, name them at all three of these levels: individual, organization, and society. For example, at the individual level: "It sounds like someone was making a racist assumption about you." At the organization level: "Sadly, I'm guessing that happens here a lot due to our history of being historically a pretty white organization." And at the society level: "I realize that it is going to take a concerted and sustained effort to shift against centuries of what we were socialized to think and do as white people in this country."

We use this ecosystem model in our workshops and acknowledge that it can all seem daunting.[2] Unquestionably, these are big challenges. Here's the good news and two encouraging reminders about how ecosystems work. First, the beauty of the Individual/Organizational/Societal model is that the influencing factors are bi-directional. Yes, Society influences your Organization and your Organization influences Individuals, but the reverse is also true. We witnessed that most vividly following the killing of George Floyd and the Black Lives Matter movement in 2020, reigniting protests, marches, and the demand for police and political reform. Second, the societal, organizational, and individual circles do not all have to be addressed at once. Sparking change within a single realm can reverberate throughout the other systems.

*Afraid to say the word "racism"?* You may have been taught not to say the words "that was racist." In trainings across organizations of all types, we frequently hear the response "Wait . . . you want me to say, 'That was racist'?! I thought I wasn't supposed to say that. I thought it was an HR violation." Take a moment to reflect on this. Naming racism would be bad? For whom? Why is it acceptable, encouraged even, to name sexism in the workplace and not name racism? This long-standing practice of teaching employees not to call out racism is itself an example of systemic racism. If we cannot use the word "racism," we cannot demand that leadership own and address the racist practices and policies within their systems. If we don't put the offensive behavior into words, it doesn't exist to the offenders. This form of erasure is very convenient for white leadership and antithetical to building inclusive organizations. Whether it is spoken or not, BIPOC within your organization are living with racism and suffering because of it. We are asking that you say "racism." We need to put words to the forces that undermine employees with rising identities. We need to name what we know is and has been happening—out loud, over and over. Don't shy away from it or assume there's no need to speak the obvious. That has never helped in the past.

Commit to ongoing reflection and action on all three levels: individual, organizational, and societal. Communicate that you realize a specific incident needs to be addressed and that the system that led to it needs to be changed by saying, "There is a lot we can do to improve things within our organization and society." Demonstrate your willingness to do the work and not rely upon or further burden employees with rising identities by asking them for the answers: "I have some ideas of things we can do, which I will continue to reflect on. If you would like to talk in the future about these ideas, just let me know. I would love to hear any ideas you have and that is not a request—as I know, it is common for people who have been oppressed to then be asked for the solution." Express your feelings in a way that keeps the focus on the Speaker: "I am so sorry that happened. It makes me sad to hear, but I am not surprised that it happened." Check in with the Speaker, and keep the door to continued dialogue open: "How are you feeling now? I will always make time to talk about things like this if you ever want to talk again." Express gratitude for the Speaker's gifts of trust, vulnerability, and openness: "Thank you for sharing this with me. I really appreciate it and feel honored that you trusted me enough to do so."

*Practicing Empowering Listening.* Let's return to the previous exchanges and swap the oppressive responses for empowering ones:

> QUEER EMPLOYEE: "I'm sad that I've never been able to vacation in a warm place in the world where I am totally comfortable holding my partner's hand. When I share this with people, I always get a list of recommendations, which I appreciate. But when I go excitedly Googling the list, I still find stats of hate crimes and recommendations against showing signs of affection in public. In some ways that hurts even more."
>
> STRAIGHT BOSS: "That sounds sad and frustrating. I like to think of myself as a strong ally and, yet, I've never given this much thought. My husband and I love Paris because it's such a romantic city. I'm sorry that you and your partner can't experience it and so many other places in the same way."
>
> EMPLOYEE WITH A PHYSICAL DISABILITY: "It seems like the parking spots designated for people with disabilities are always full by the time I arrive at 8 a.m."
>
> ABLE-BODIED SUPERVISOR: "I'm embarrassed to admit this, but everyone complains so much around here about the parking. It never occurred to me how much more challenging it could be for you and my other staff with disabilities. I imagine it's really frustrating to navigate every day and hurtful that no one even mentions it. Thank you for bringing something to my attention that I should have paid closer attention to. That's not okay."
>
> GAY EMPLOYEE: "Coming out was really hard and caused a lot of tension in my family for years."
>
> STRAIGHT EMPLOYEE: "It really makes me feel sad to even imagine you going through that with your family for so many years. If you ever want to talk more about it, I'm here to listen."

BLACK EMPLOYEE: "It's discouraging to see that Kimberly, who is of African heritage, has stayed in the same position in the company for five years while Amanda, who is white, has been promoted twice in less time."

WHITE SUPERVISOR: "Thank you for speaking with me about the contrast. I'm not at liberty to speak about specific personnel issues, but I can definitely understand how seeing white employees advancing more quickly than employees of color is discouraging. I also know that there is evidence showing that is a common trend across industries. As we have so few directors of color, your questions and feelings are perfectly valid and I appreciate you starting this dialogue with me. I will commit to looking into potential patterns across our organization."

FEMALE EMPLOYEE: "When I participated on that national panel last week, they introduced all of the male panelists by their titles and called me by my first name. It felt weird."

MALE EMPLOYEE: "That sounds sexist and disrespectful. I'm sorry that happened to you and suspect it wasn't the first time. How are you feeling now? Do you want to talk more about it?"

*Brenda and the task force.* A colleague shared the following story about the potential healing and organizational growth that can occur through Empowering Listening. In the aftermath of George Floyd's murder, Brenda's CEO asked her to serve on a small task force charged with addressing racism and promoting justice. What occurred during their hastily convened inaugural meeting would set the course for the work to come. The charge was straightforward: develop an action plan that would detail steps toward eliminating racism and promoting justice and health equity within their predominantly white organization and in the community. There was only one problem: Brenda was physically and emotionally exhausted. Since the start of the pandemic and as an expert in her field, she eagerly had accepted invitations to give talks, conduct workshops, join panels, coauthor papers, and speak with the media about issues at the intersection of race, ethnicity, a public health crisis, international unrest, protests, and emotional well-being. As a Black, queer, cisgender manager, Brenda had been managing her own feelings of marginalization while supporting others within the company for years. Against this backdrop, she was coping with a few personal, distressing, and yet to be resolved identity-related aggressions, which had recently occurred at work.

The task force meeting began with a vengeance as strategies, interventions, and recommendations poured forth from this talented and productive team. Then, all of a sudden, according to Brenda, she had a rare (as in first-ever) out-of-body experience in the workplace. The proverbial dam broke. Brenda shared her frustration and disillusionment with her task force colleagues, who were white and straight. She provided examples of recent identity-related aggressions. She spoke candidly about her exhaustion and the disconnect she was feeling between the task force's charge and her lived experience. She expressed her unwillingness to participate on yet another committee that would merely check a box. She spoke about wanting to promote a more honest reckoning with racism and marginalization within their company. Finally, Brenda admitted that even if her colleagues could commit to a reenvisioned charge, she didn't know how much she had left to give.

Remarkably, her colleagues listened. Instantaneously, the tremendous urgency to meet the charge and produce deliverables was paused. They paused to listen. They paused to validate. They paused to understand. They paused to convey empathy. They offered Brenda support, time, and space to decide how she wanted to proceed with the task force and they thanked her for sharing the truth about her experiences. Brenda recounts that the pausing made her wonder, *Am I in the eye of the hurricane? What's coming next?* The meeting ended, and what *did* come next was that all of the listening, gratitude, and empathy extended to her during the meeting was expressed again, individually and in writing, by every member of the task force. They extended offers to connect again one-on-one. They said things like "I know your plate is very full right now. When you're ready, I want you to know that I would really like to speak with you. Maybe have a so-cially distanced cup of tea?" and "It took so much courage to say what you did. I'm so grateful that you did. Thank you." They recommitted to the work with a shared sense of purpose, fully acknowledging the opportunities and barriers that awaited.

Brenda's story illustrates what can happen when trust and Em-powering Listening meet up in the workplace. Not only did Brenda decide to remain, but she was asked to lead the task force efforts in a way that felt appreciated and supported. Additionally, the team successfully obtained additional financial compensation for her ef-forts, acknowledging the difficult load of doing this work while Black. Together, the team generated a comprehensive and robust action plan that acknowledged the "head and heart" sweat equity and per-sistence it would take to transform their organization's relationship to race, justice, and equity. The organization set the action plan as the highest priority and identified funding to implement the team's recommendations.

*Consider a Listening Tour.* Once you have trained members of the organization who are adept at Empowering Listening, consider initi-ating a Listening Tour. Research tells us that when top leaders make themselves available to hear the experiences of those who have felt marginalized, invisible, or oppressed, a shift toward a more inclusive culture can take place.[3] Listening Tours can take many forms, but in short they are a series of structured focus groups or conversations intended to create space where the entire system acknowledges that oppression exists within the organization and collects stories and examples of how those forces have played out. When some degree of trust and Empowering Listening converge within the designated space, organizational culture can move toward becoming more just, equitable, and inclusive. Leaders can learn more about the condi-tion of the organization relative to identity-related aggressions and inclusivity, which presents opportunities for growth and change. The Listening Tour is initiated with an expressed commitment from leadership to learn about and address all forms of oppression in the workplace. Begin by identifying the Listeners. These are often people within the institution who hold power. It is paramount that those selected are trained on how to listen. Training typically involves required prereading materials, a didactic seminar on listening strategies, and skills practice. Once Listeners have been trained, they embark on a series of listening events across the organization, divided by unit, by groups at certain levels, and/or by employee identities. Inviting former trainees or students who have graduated from an institution can be especially illuminating, as these individuals are intimately familiar with the culture and may feel less encumbered by organizational position. Listening Sessions are structured to empower the Speakers, those who courageously step forward to share their experiences of the workplace. Speakers are invited and encouraged to take the majority of space in the room, while Listeners are encouraged to validate, reflect, and commit to thinking about ways they can change the organization to address issues expressed.

In our work we have found it helpful to include a third role: that of Observer. Ideally, the Observers are more practiced at Empowering Listening and can offer in-the-moment or post-session feedback to the Listeners about how they can continue to identify and lessen their spots of low awareness, avoid typical Oppressive Listening traps, and hone their Empowering Listening skills. After each listening session, Speakers, Listeners, and Observers are asked to respond to a structured survey summarizing their experience. In this survey, it can be helpful to document themes that were shared and heard, evaluate both the quality and quantity of listening, and note listening skills that were employed as well as those in need of improvement. Importantly, the post-survey is where leaders can begin to document the action ideas, recommendations, and next steps they skillfully withheld during the Listening session. Following the Listening Tour, Listeners debrief with trainers to discuss findings and changes to be integrated into the organization's strategic plan for becoming more just and equitable.

Oppressive Listening shuts down conversation and discourages further sharing. In contrast, Empowering Listening creates pockets of space where people can come together across identities and positionality within the organization to build understanding of the ways that people with rising identities are oppressed. By creating an environment that empowers the Speaker, we not only build a community that can work together to dismantle problematic systems; we create a workplace in which someone with a rising identity can envision a healthier and, therefore, sustainable tenure. We build diverse teams that sustain and empower all within the organization.

# CHAPTER 9

# STAYING SAFE: SWIMMING IN THE SCHOOL

· Salima's Story ·

*Salima was a muslim, cisgender, female pilot of south Asian and Black heritage who was fluent in four languages. Less than a decade ago, she was writing for Howard University's law review as a first-year student while also pursuing her MBA in the university's prestigious joint program. Now, she was poised to crack the glass ceiling of the airline industry. Those closest to Salima had nicknamed her "the Hamilton of the South" because of the tireless work ethic and sense of urgency she brought to all pursuits. She didn't love the moniker, but she understood exactly how she earned the comparison. It was gratifying to her that so many mentees and colleagues of diverse identities seemed to take pride in her accomplishments, as if they readily could see themselves reflected in her. Though she was well respected by those in her close circle, that did not generalize to the airport staff, who routinely asked her a few extra questions at security while her white peers flashed their badges for half a second and strolled on by. Once, a new TSA employee pulled a manager aside and Salima overheard the whisper: "I think we've got a fake-badge situation here." Salima practiced standing tall and proud, focusing on what she knew would soon come: red cheeks and a flurry of apologies.*

*With each new incident, however, Salima is growing more impatient and restless. At work, where she's known for her unflappable manner, her irritability is getting more difficult to contain. Her poker face is beginning to crack and only she knows why. It's the holy month of Ramadan. Salima has been successful with her fasting but hasn't come close to meeting the five daily prayers and spiritual reflection encouraged by her faith. She's grown weary of the negative stereotypes and relentless paranoia enveloping her at work and, predictably, these feelings intensify during the holiday. In her industry, the religious bias has been inescapable. From airline policies to complaints and slurs that flow freely from both colleagues and customers, there is no respite. Certainly, Salima is no shrinking violet, but she has learned to pace herself and choose her battles carefully in the workplace. Rather than address every utterance or identity-related aggression, she has chosen to fight the bigotry at the policy level, where she can effect lasting change. Salima didn't consciously decide not to share her faith with colleagues, but for whatever reason, people assumed it was okay to make disparaging remarks in her presence. "This must be what it's like to pass for white," she sometimes joked with her friends. She couldn't help but wonder how she would be judged if her colleagues knew that she was a person who possesses another "hidden" rising identity. Two years ago, she was diagnosed with multiple sclerosis. Now her gait, once steady and sure, is beginning to betray a progressive illness that she has worked hard to forestall. In her young but meteoric career, she has witnessed repeatedly that, like Muslims, people with disabilities are often on the receiving end of bias and insults. Indeed, Salima has been working like she was running out of time. "Hamilton of the South?" she chuckled softly to herself. If they only knew.*

## STICKING WITH THE SCHOOL

Salima has not only survived but *thrived* in this workplace by learning to "swim in the school." Often, individuals with rising identities suppress their thoughts, opinions, and experiences, both internally and externally, to feel safe, gain acceptance, and succeed in an organization. In doing so, individuals who might feel, look, and experience things very differently from those around them can camouflage themselves and be perceived as part of the "in-group." Unfortunately, we humans tend to gravitate toward those we perceive to be like us. Thus, we often buff out the edges that make us unique so we can be perceived as "normal" and sometimes "palatable" in the workplace.

Even if the long-term goal is to make change within the organization, individuals often have to first learn to swim with the school, despite the marginalization and pain that inherently come with suppressing one's authentic self. Individuals must first "earn their stripes" and advance within the school before they can eventually suggest slight tweaks to the direction in which the fish are swimming. For example, Lauren suppressed her sexual orientation at many workplaces before feeling that she had built up enough idiosyncrasy credits (a social psychology term describing an individual's ability to deviate from group expectations and still be accepted) to absorb the professional hit that might come with sharing an identity that some dislike. Even after coming out, Lauren waited a few months before starting to advocate for revisions to make intake forms more inclusive for LGBTQIA+ people. Similarly, Stephanie waited until the leadership respected her expertise as a director before offering constructive criticism as to how the organization could improve related to DEI. By swimming along with the school, and showing the bigger fish (the ones with the power and privilege) your worth, you gain some leverage to slowly change the direction in which the school is swimming. Each time you suggest a change of course, there is a risk of it not going well, which might cost a big deduction in your Workplace Social Capital. If the suggestion goes well, or your standing within the organization is solid, you can accrue more Workplace Social Capital over time to prepare to suggest the next change.

In addition to holding back opinions until one has accrued power within the organization, swimming in the stream for people who identify as African American often involves some level of code-switching, the act of adjusting your speech based on who you are speaking to. Code-switching is most often used to describe the different ways that many African American people speak or dress, for example, depending on who is in the room. We will discuss code-switching in greater depth in chapter 13, on creating an anti-racist organization.

Code-switching, and other forms of identity suppression, can go beyond words. For example, when in environments perceived as unsafe, Lauren might identity-suppress by subtly shifting the conversation away from topics such as "What did you do this weekend?" or "Are you planning on having kids?" so she does not have to disclose or actively hide that she is married to a woman. A cisgender man might enjoy wearing dresses but choose not to when at work to avoid eliciting discomfort among coworkers. A person interviewing for a position might choose not to use their wheelchair the day of the interview, even against medical advice, to avoid being perceived as "weak." Eventually, if these individuals accrue enough power within the organization to comfortably come out and share their perspectives, they may be able to insist on cultural reform and propel the institution to be more inclusive.

Unfortunately, in most organizations the ease with which you are accepted into the stream and your required levels of identity suppression (code-switching) most likely relate to how far your identities, and expression of those identities, stand apart from societal expectations, dominant norms, and stereotypes. For example, across communities of color there are a multitude of differences. Two women might share the same dark complexion but white people are likely to respond differently to each if one identifies as African American and the other is a first-generation Nigerian immigrant. White people might compliment the Black employee with straight hair for how "professional" she looks and penalize the Black colleague who prefers braids, headwraps, or hairstyles popular for more kinky or textured hair. People who identify as Asian American and Asian immigrants are often beneficiaries—or targets—of the model minority myth (in addition to many negative stereotypes), which stereotypes them as law-abiding citizens of the United States who are more successful at "pulling themselves up by their bootstraps" compared to other marginalized racial and ethnic groups. We also know that there is light-skinned privilege (shadeism) within and outside of the communities of color (Latinx, Afro-Latinx, South Asian, Asian, Black), under which individuals with lighter skin are often given access to historically white spaces and associated power before their darker-skinned colleagues. Having lighter skin also can come with insidious denial of Black identity both within and outside of the Black community, such as Malik's experience in chapter 6.

## WHY THIS IS A PROBLEM

Sure, we all swim in the stream to some extent when we start a new job. We hold off on recommending the company switch to a better service for document sharing or revealing our true thoughts on how we feel about Tom's staff meeting agendas. However, repressing one's thoughts and behaviors when it comes to identities can be especially emotionally draining and harmful. Setting aside one's sense of self and personhood to make it through the day, get a paycheck, and build a career creates an extraordinary and profound type of exhaustion. The psychological and physical consequences are well documented and real. We know there are benefits and dangers to not being "out." For example, we know that while staying closeted as gay reduces instances of outright discrimination, it also increases depression and anxiety. Coming out, on the flip side, comes with risk of job loss, workplace discrimination, and, in certain contexts, homelessness and family rejection. This can feel like an awful tradeoff.

Staying safe while swimming in the stream can sometimes feel like you've been cast in a *Get Out* scenario.[1] Even though you are the one being marginalized, it can appear to others that you are complacent and perfectly okay with all that is or isn't happening. You can feel like a hypocrite when you support the work of a marginalizing supervisor, especially after confiding in your trusted group about the long list of the supervisor's identity-related aggressions you have witnessed.

This need for suppression of identity and social justice advocacy exists because organizations historically have been run by people without rising identities. The slow cycle of swimming, then turning, then swimming, then turning the school causes change to be painfully slow and makes burnout the norm. This is the opposite of a sustainably diverse organization.

## WHAT TO DO ABOUT IT

*For the school.* Staying safe while swimming in the stream is unacceptable and a waste of precious human resources. Leadership should recognize this dynamic and that their company is not immune to it. This is a leadership problem, and it needs to be addressed by them. Leaders, you should not put this book down and go ask "if this is a thing" within your organization. Take it from us—it is. Consider naming the dynamic in a town hall or a letter to your company. Acknowledge who has historically held power within your organization. Admit how a lack of diverse identities among leadership has led to a limited understanding of how to create an inclusive and sustainable experience for various types of people. For example, your business may be owned by a Black woman, but how many of your employees are openly trans* or gender nonconforming? How many have disabilities? Bring in training for leadership that is tailored to increase your cultural awareness and humility in working with people who bring an expanded range of identities. Invest in training in which giving and receiving feedback across differences and identities is practiced, such as an Empowering Listening tour that takes place every six months for the foreseeable future.

Identify those in your organization who have shared rising identities and have demonstrated investment in your organization. For example, can you think of people who have tried to point out identity-related issues in the workplace for the sake of elevating the company? Can you think of employees with rising identities who bring their full selves to work, or close to it, and who work to develop meaningful friendships across identities? Has anyone offered suggestions on how the company could reorganize the space in a way that's more accessible for those with physical disabilities? Offer individuals like these professional development, promotions, and leadership opportunities. Give them platforms to speak, and really listen to what they say. Observe and learn from them how they manage within the organization and seek to educate others while skillfully "staying safe." Notice the subtle ways in which they are attempting to give your organization the gift of insight. Remember that they are trying to help you and your organization catch this wave of change. Reward them for their work, skill, and commitment and for choosing to invest in your organization.

*For the fish.* Individuals who find themselves swimming in the stream need to know and trust that this is not their problem to fix. However, there are ways to make the swimming more sustainable, discussed here and in chapter 12, "Sustaining Yourself." Like mastering the breaststroke, you can learn to swim in a more sustainable way. First, remind yourself often that "staying safe while swimming in the stream" definitely is a thing. This phenomenon is very common among underrepresented identities within organizations. You are not alone. If your experience is like ours, most organizations you have worked in were probably not created by people who share your marginalized identities.

Second, identify the pain that exists at the intersection of your identities, the way your organization was built, and the failings of those within it. Identify and name your feelings about this three-way intersection and give yourself permission to feel sadness, anger, shame, or a combination of the above. Remind yourself that this pain you are feeling is not due to a problem inherent in you. There is nothing wrong with you. You are not overly sensitive; you are aware. You are not whiny; you are brave. You are not making this up; you are attempting to thrive and to help others to do the same. Place the pain where it belongs: on society. Practice saying statements like "This pain I am feeling is not my fault. It is the result of living in a racist society that was built in a way that undermines my true worth and abilities." Find social support, within and outside of the organization. Find people with whom you can vent—have your experiences validated and be reminded that this is not okay. Your organization is *really* fortunate to have you.

When learning to shift the tide most effectively, it is important to get a grasp on the politics within the organization: Who is in charge? Who clearly has power to openly speak their mind? Who has power to quietly influence the tide? Who, along with you, is trying to shift the institution's direction? Being aware of the complexities of power and politics can reveal multiple avenues for encouraging change.

You can choose to turn the tide in a number of ways. You can press for change privately and quietly, particularly if you anticipate that leadership might be defensive or explosive, or might retaliate in response. If private attempts have not been successful, you may find that public pressure elicits faster change. You can turn the tide by being outspoken and advocating for change, calling out injustice within your organization. Demands might include listing the issues and asking leadership to address them with external consultants, offering specific ways you think they could fix the issues, or a combination of the two.

Another way to turn the tide is to work through your relationships within the organization. By slowly cultivating your relationships and gradually sharing more of yourself, your identities, and related experiences, you can inspire change by increasing your colleagues' understanding of your reality. Most likely, their increased understanding will be accompanied by empathy and compassion. If you are able to build trusting relationships—with both those who do and do not share your identities—you may foster energy, enthusiasm, and commitment to change far beyond what you alone can bring. This approach takes vulnerability but can lead to the powerful formation of multiple, steadfast agents of change throughout the organization. As a side benefit, these people also might become trusted emotional supports for you.

Finally, you can also turn the tide by reinforcing positive behaviors. For instance, we find acknowledgment of our work and appreciation of our contributions to be rewarding. We even find hearing our own names rewarding. So note and acknowledge small moments when colleagues are engaging in desired actions (such as when someone points out to a fellow researcher that they should use the term "white" instead of "Caucasian"; see "A Few Tips to Go" after the glossary for a description of why if this distinction is new to you, as it is to many). Encourage those actions publicly, privately, or both by celebrating them and sharing your appreciation. Celebrating others' improvements will encourage them to feel empowered and inspired by the work. The good news is, this tide is turning. And whether organizations like it or not, they will be expected to demonstrate the ability to sustain their diverse workforces. We look forward to the time when "staying safe while swimming in the school" is no longer a reality in many organizations.

# CHAPTER 10

# RESPONDING TO IDENTITY-RELATED
# AGGRESSIONS (IRAS)

THE NEGATIVE EFFECTS OF IDENTITY-RELATED AGGRESSIONS (also referred to as IRAs or microaggressions) have surfaced repeatedly throughout this book. Here, we revisit "pioneers" Seth, Chris, and Roxanne from chapter 3 to review and illustrate specific strategies for responding to these pervasive and hurtful behaviors at both individual and systemic levels.

*Teach and practice upstander and allyship skills.* In order for firsts of any rising identity to thrive in organizations where their identities are underrepresented, upstanders and allies need to be skilled and in place to greet them. A bystander can be anyone who witnesses or is aware of unjust behavior or practices and deems them worthy of comment or action.[1] The word "upstander" was derived from the term bystander and refers to one who takes a stand against these injustices. Dr. Derald Wing Sue, who has written extensively about the impact of microaggressions in the workplace and other settings, defines racial microaggressions as "the everyday slights, indignities, putdowns, and insults that minorities experience in their day-to-day interactions with well-intentioned individuals who are unaware that they have engaged in an offensive act or made an offensive statement." Sue and his colleagues recently published a framework for addressing micro-aggressions.[2] Their strategic approach offers "concrete action steps and dialogues (referred to as micro-interventions) that targets, allies and bystanders can perform." The proposed micro-interventions are organized into the four strategic goals, listed below. We have applied them to Seth's scenario and offered an upstander's possible range of responses. For reasons detailed in chapter 3, we have replaced the term "microaggressions" with "identity-related aggressions," or IRAs.

*Scenario:* An African American, male student (Seth) is approached in class by a white teaching assistant who asks if he is the student who has been failing to show up to the course's study section. The student he is looking for is white.

*Metacommunication:* Black students are more likely than their white peers not to meet their academic obligations and to slack off.

The professor, who is white, overhears the exchange, seizes the upstander moment, and approaches the teaching assistant. He might do so using one or a combination of the following strategies:

*Make the invisible visible.* If the encounter feels like it is about race—if you get that awful feeling in your stomach—it likely is. Name the racism. Make it real by putting it right out there on the table: "It appears you may have assumed that because Seth is Black and a student-athlete, he is the underperforming student in your section. Any student in this lecture hall, regardless of race, could be the student you're looking for." Notice how to name racist behavior. The professor did not have to say, "You're a racist," a phrase many white people are afraid of. Instead, the professor offered that the teaching assistant *appeared* to be acting in line with the racist socialization that taught him to categorize for easier comprehension of the world. In this example the professor is "calling in" the teaching assistant, offering him insight into a likely unseen corner of his thinking. The professor does not have to use a scolding voice; he can be calm and warm while suggesting a quick shift in the teaching assistant's thinking and inviting further conversation. Ideally the teaching assistant would take some time to work through the understandable embarrassment and other emotions that emerge, and eventually continue the conversation with the professor. Most likely the professor or upstander will need to keep leading the way by offering this white affinity space—a space for white people to process together—to explore the ways they are enacting how they were socialized to think about Black people.

*Disarm the identity-related aggression.* Questions are a powerful way to disarm identity-related aggressions. Questions bring about a pause in this fast-paced world and create opportunities for people to reflect and delve into their words and actions. In Seth's classroom example, the professor could say, "It sounds like you are looking for a student who has been slacking off. I wonder why out of 150 mostly white students in this lecture hall, you thought it was a Black student who wasn't meeting the course requirements?" Asking a question puts the onus on the aggressor to explore why the identity-related aggression happened. Depending on the context, relationship, and setting, disarming might be most effective in the moment or in a private space, one on one, at a later time. Consider who is watching. Is the whole first row of the lecture hall watching how this unfolds? Is the room still relatively empty ten minutes before the class starts? Do you have time to check in with both parties immediately following class? Does this aggressor tend to act out when uncomfortable? Do they have more or less power within the organization? These factors can inform how best to intervene.

The disarming-questions strategy is excellent following a joke made at the expense of a rising group. For example, if you are standing at the watercooler and your colleague approaches you, glances at the new gender-queer employee making themselves coffee, and says, "Look! It drinks coffee just like the rest of us!" you might respond quickly with "Can you explain why that is funny? I don't understand." This strategy is especially effective in helping move through that "deer in the headlights" feeling, as you can practice and plan to use this exact sentence following any identity-related joke.

*Educate the perpetrator.* Providing education about stereotypes is an act of kindness, as it acknowledges that not everyone has been taught to see the destructive patterns. Taking the time to educate can also depersonalize the responsibility for having been taught to see the world through racial stereotypes. Note the stark contrast between "You're a racist" and "You, just like me, were taught to see the world in a way that categorizes people inaccurately." The professor in this example might say, "You might not realize this, but what just occurred demonstrates a common negative stereotype of Black students. Seth has never missed a section and is one of the top-performing students in this class. Assuming that he is the student that has been slacking off based on his appearance is not okay. Racial stereotypes are not acceptable in this class or institution." Again, the professor can use a warm and inviting tone, signaling that he suspects it was not the teaching assistant's goal to treat Seth in a hurtful way. However, the professor is firm, setting clear limits and expectations for conduct. The professor could go on to explore how the teaching assistant would like to move forward. Would it make sense to talk to Seth and apologize? Could this be done in a way that would not further burden Seth? Would the teaching assistant like a list of resources to explore these concepts further? Is it the professor's duty to provide these regardless of the teaching assistant's level of interest?

*Seek (or provide) external reinforcement or support.* If we want to change the often invisible ways that systems oppress people, we need to continuously strive to amplify and illustrate through words. We must not shy away from naming racism, sexism, ableism, and other prejudices when we see them. In this example, the professor could approach Seth directly, saying, "I want you to know that I saw what just happened, and it is not okay. It looked like he was acting out of stereotyped beliefs, as I know you have been at every class, which is so unusual for a morning lecture! I am going to speak with the teaching assistant about the harm of racial stereotypes. How are you doing and is there anything else I can do in response to this incident?"

Notice the many interventions packed into this statement. First, the professor took the responsibility to name what was wrong. He didn't say, "What the heck? You've been here every class—why would he think you are Nathaniel?" Asking Seth that question would likely exacerbate the insult by making him feel either invisible in his race-related pain, responsible for educating the professor, or both. Instead, the professor called it out for what it was, clearly and concisely. He did not go on and on lamenting racism, subjecting Seth to his white processing of the subject. He also identified a strength in Seth that is counter to the stereotype that was enacted. He pointed out how hard-working and committed to school Seth is, and complimented him for it. Next, he committed to action. He had already thought of what he will do next and shares that with Seth. While he did ask Seth if there was anything additional he could do in response to the incident, he offered his idea first. Resisting the natural tendency to ask Seth to generate next steps and offering him a space to share any ideas if he would like to was an impactful but frequently overlooked intervention. Depending on the moment, the professor might offer to speak later or convey that his door is always open to discuss this or related incidents and themes. The professor might even go a step further in providing support based upon his scholarship and academic performance. At the end of the course, he could approach Seth and tell him he would be happy to offer him a teaching assistantship or write a letter of recommendation for future positions or graduate school applications. By doing so, the professor would be offering his privilege and power to help propel Seth's career, another way he could directly counter stereotypes faced by African American students.

*Strategies for targets of identity-related aggressions.* In this section we apply Sue's model to a range of responses that the person who has been targeted can make. When working with those who are on the receiving end of IRAs, we always start by emphasizing this key point: remember that the W's (as Stephanie calls them) of responding to these incidents are yours to decide; stand firm and center yourself by pausing to think, *The choice of Whether, When, or Where I respond, and What to say, if anything, is entirely mine to make.* No one gets to dictate what *should* be done in any given situation. IRAs can be very challenging to interpret in the moment and frequently are accompanied by strong feelings. Breathe. Remove the pressure to generate the perfect response. The goal in developing these skills isn't to come up with the ideal, mic-drop reply. There is no such thing. Rather, approach these situations as opportunities to grow and to take care of yourself and, when you opt to do so, to enlighten others and promote their growth as well.

*Scenario:* An African American young woman, Roxanne, boards an aircraft and places her bag in the overhead bin. The white flight attendant steps forward to explain that the bin she is using is reserved for first-class passengers only. Only seconds before, the young white female passenger who had boarded just before Roxanne placed her baggage in the first-class bin before heading to her seat in coach.

*Metacommunication:* Black passengers can't afford to purchase a seat in the most expensive section of the aircraft. Black passengers don't follow the rules of the airline.

*Make the invisible visible.* Roxanne might very well choose to continue to get settled into her seat before saying anything at all, especially since boarding a flight is often a frenzied procedure. She could ring the call button at any point during the flight to speak with the attendant or even walk over to where she is sitting once passengers are free to move about the aircraft. Making the invisible visible is a clear statement of the metacommunication as she perceived it: "It appears that you made certain assumptions about where I belong on this airplane because of my race. Did you happen to notice that the white woman who boarded just ahead of me did, in fact, place her bag in the first-class overhead bin although her seat is in coach? Black people can and do purchase first-class tickets, and for you, an airline representative, to assume otherwise is problematic."

*Disarming the identity-related aggression.* The target can choose from among several options for disarming IRAs. For young adults who may be early in their skill development, asking questions can be an excellent place to begin. In this instance Roxanne might adopt a curious stance by saying, "Oh, good morning [smiling]. My name is Roxanne and this is my seat. I wonder why you assumed otherwise?" As discussed previously, asking questions creates a moment for pause and reflection on the part of the aggressor. For the target who is Black (or identity-fatigued), asking questions can provide a welcome break from the emotional burden of educating the aggressor or making the invisible visible. Roxanne's disarming smile and greeting demonstrate a version of a skill frequently taught in psychology called "opposite action." Opposite action involves choosing to do exactly the opposite of what your emotions are telling you to do, particularly in charged situations. Had Roxanne expressed anger and frustration, those emotions would have been perfectly valid. However, over time the negative emotions triggered by IRAs will tax Roxanne's mental and physical health.[3] Had she been traveling with a colleague, her professional reputation may have taken a hit as well. The opposite action skill is another skill to keep in your toolkit for preservation of health and professional reputation.

Using this same approach, Seth might have adopted a curious stance by saying, "Hmm, sounds like you're looking for a student who's been slacking off. I wonder why out of the 150 students in the lecture hall you thought it was me?" Or more directly: "That's fascinating that you 'thought he looked like me.' I wonder what made you think that?" Posing a question can be regarded as the insertion of a semicolon into an identity-related aggression, giving the target and aggressor the option of returning to explore further together or separately, or not.

## EDUCATE THE PERPETRATOR

*Seek (or provide) external reinforcement or support.* At this point there is a twist in Roxanne's story. She did not have to look far for external reinforcement or support. It turns out that an older Black woman, who was boarding the flight just behind her, had observed the scenario and immediately stepped into the upstander role. First, try to imagine being a witness to this situation, watching the scene unfold before you, as you hurry to board. Would you have picked up on the IRA even if you didn't share Roxanne's racial identity? Next, see if you can generate a response using at least one of the four approaches. Roxanne's upstander did not hesitate. She spoke directly with the flight attendant and calmly asked to speak with her supervisor. Her response employed three of the four strategies: making the invisible visible, educating the perpetrator, and seeking external reinforcement. Perhaps most important, Roxanne's upstander modeled a highly skilled response and the power of addressing IRAs head-on for Roxanne and any would-be upstanders. We hope others took note.

*When you are the aggressor.* You might be inclined to skip this section, thinking, *I've never perpetrated an identity-related aggression in my life* or perhaps, *I'm pretty good at taking responsibility for my actions. Besides, admitting mistakes and making sincere apologies are strengths of mine.* We encourage you to keep reading because, whether we realize it or not, we have all engaged in IRAs and we all will again. Even if you typically are the target or upstander, we encourage you to keep reading. Regardless of role, the ability to deliver and recognize an appropriate response to IRAs is a necessary skill set to have if you want to develop healthy relationships across identities.

*The Oppressive Apology.* As discussed in chapter 7, an appropriate apology maintains focus on and prioritizes the needs of the person who has been targeted and marginalized. Like with Empowering Listening, the goal is to shift power away from the aggressor toward the target. Here are the common markers that can help you to recognize and rein in oppressive apologies.

When confronted with the knowledge that we have committed an identity-related aggression, it is natural to feel shame or guilt and, accordingly, to respond defensively. We tend to spend a lot of time (error one: taking too long) explaining (error two: acting from defensiveness, making excuses) why we said what we said (error three: unnecessary focus on the aggressor) and what we intended (error four: focusing on the intention versus impact). The Oppressive Apology continues with assertions that we never intended to hurt or offend anyone (a repeat of error four) and shifts focus to the aggressor's feelings (error five: claiming the emotional space). We might go on and on with statements like "I feel *so* bad about this," "I'm *so* sorry; I just feel awful," or "I couldn't concentrate on my work because I was so upset about what happened." We might do so with intense eye contact, searching for signs of forgiveness. We might even overtly ask for forgiveness or understanding (error six: asking the person in pain to exert even more emotional labor to soothe the aggressor). These sneaky but common behaviors—errors one through six—only serve to increase the burden on the individual who has already been oppressed by your actions.

The Oppressive Apology asks the person who has been marginalized to sit there and listen, perhaps maintaining a neutral-to-warm facial expression, while you take the stage. The Oppressive Apology asks the targeted person to ignore their feelings while listening to your story about why you said what you said and describe your privilege and lack of awareness of your blind spots. Worse, although you may have just been enlightened, they are likely already well aware. It is hurtful and insulting for the target to be reminded of how and why you've never had to think about racism, sexism, homophobia, or ableism. The Oppressive Apology asks the target to take care of the aggressor and their feelings at the exact time when the target's feelings should be acknowledged and addressed. Finally, the Oppressive Apology asks the other person to resolve the aggressor's discomfort, anxiety, shame, or guilt by agreeing that the interaction is complete: "We're all good here. Right?" This undermines the weight of an IRA and suggests that these things can be "done" or checked off a list.

That's far from the truth, as the impacts of receiving an IRA can last days, months, or even years.

There is one more characteristic of the Oppressive Apology and it is especially egregious. This error typically surfaces after the aggressor has had a little time to consider how they might make amends. In these scenarios, the oppressive apologizer presents "opportunities" for the marginalized, aggressed person to educate others. These opportunities come in many forms, such as asking the target to provide trainings, presentations, panels, workshops, professional talks, grand rounds, staff in-services, and white papers. These invitations reinforce the painful and unacceptable pattern of relying upon the most underrepresented and marginalized within the organization to educate the very system that has oppressed them by explaining what should already be known and how to improve. It is all just too much.

*The Empowering Apology.* The Empowering Apology, first and foremost, seeks to empower the targeted individual(s) and is mindful of the additional burden one is placing on those who were marginalized in the situation. The Empowering Apology suppresses the sometimes overwhelming urge to attend to the needs of the aggressor in the moment. This approach skips the part where we share our feelings of hurt and clarify our intention. The Empowering Apology is succinct. This approach might involve asking in advance if the person would be open to hearing an apology and if so, what their preferred method would be. In person? In writing?

Returning to Roxanne's interaction, the flight attendant might simply say, "That was inappropriate and hurtful. I'm very sorry," or "I apologize and commit to learning from what just took place. Thank you for taking the time and energy to speak with me. You didn't have to and I'm grateful that you did." If the flight attendant is met with silence, she should carry and process that anxiety on her own or with another white person. In Seth's situation, the teaching assistant might check in with him after class by saying, "I realize that my assumption was racist. I'm very sorry," or "I'd like the opportunity to apologize for my hurtful and biased actions. If you are open to it, please let me know whether you'd prefer sitting down together or a written message from me. Whatever your decision, thank you for making me aware." A vital component of the Empowering Apology is the expression of gratitude to the person who just gave you the gift of feedback. Remember to say "thank you."

*Training the organization to recognize and disarm IRAs.* Fortunately, there are excellent resources, trainings, and experts that organizations can consult to address IRAs systemically. For example, the Restorative Justice Center at the University of California Berkeley offers workshops and trainings on restorative practices and restorative justice for people at UCB, on campuses around the country, and in Bay Area communities. Restorative justice practitioners believe that when harm occurs (as with IRAs), the ways of taking accountability for that harm should result in both repair and transformation. Restorative practices emphasize harm reduction and prevention through storytelling, empathy, and social and emotional learning. Hollaback! is a global nonprofit whose mission is to end harassment in all of its forms by transforming the culture that perpetuates it. Their original focus was to end gender-based harassment in public spaces, and in 2015 they expanded their efforts to end harassment across all spaces and identities, including women, LGBTQIA+ people, Black people, Indigenous people, people of color, religious minorities, people with disabilities, immigrants, and others who are treated as "less than" just for being who they are. Hollaback! employs a train-the-trainer model through which trainers receive ongoing education and support.

We recommend that organizations take time to identify a systemic approach that will align with their needs. It is important to meet your workforce where the majority are developmentally. If the training is too basic, your employees will be bored and lose interest. If it's too advanced, people will feel intimidated and anxious. Consider conducting a workforce survey or needs assessment to gain a better understanding of the cultural responsiveness of your staff. Feedback and scenarios unearthed through a Listening Tour (see chapter 8) can be very instructive. Experiences reported during the tour can be used to inform the training for disarming IRAs, which, in turn, heightens the authenticity and salience for participants. In our work we find that organizations can get stalled at this juncture. Months and even years can be lost while searching for the perfect training. A word of caution here: don't allow perfection to be the enemy of the good. Set a deadline by which you will commit to next steps for training the organization to disarm identity-related aggressions and stick to it. (See chapter 11 for strategies for promoting staff engagement before trainings are introduced.)

*Coalition-building for change.* We often speak with individuals who would like their companies to engage a systemic-change initiative but don't necessarily hold power within their system. As our schools and workplaces become more diverse, they often do so from the bottom up. We typically first see increased diversity among the roles and levels that have the least amount of power, such as interns, first-year college students, and those in entry-level positions. This growth pattern means that three discordant factors converge: those with little decision-making power and influence (like Jaymie in chapter 1) are enduring the most IRAs and tend to be the most motivated to bring training and change to the organization. Thus, when they choose to act, these individuals assume the greatest personal and professional risk.

If you find yourself at this crossroad, we have several recommendations for you. First, reflect on whether you want to make the request for your organization to change by name or anonymously. Unfortunately, pushing for inclusiveness and equity can be risky. If you hold rising identities while asking for change, leadership could defensively brush off your request and label you as "too sensitive." If you decide to remain anonymous, consider writing a letter describing the specific behaviors and interactions you have witnessed and what you think needs to change. You may mask your identity by claiming you are someone with privileged identities, writing, for instance, "As a white, heterosexual man, I have seen many harmful things happen to our employees of color." In addition to bringing you an additional layer of protection, sadly, this approach has the added benefit of making the letter more valid to leadership if they also identify as white and straight. You might simply slip this book, or books such as *White Fragility* and *Black Fatigue*, under the doors of top leaders of the organization.

If you choose to speak out by name, consider doing so with allies and other advocates by your side. See if you can create a diverse team of people who hold a range of rising and privileged identities to make a statement or request together. You might reach out to people who seem safe and share some examples of what you have observed or experienced (IRAs, higher turnover among BIPOC employees) and what you think can be done, such as restorative justice training. You could invite these colleagues to join the cause or to sign a statement by name or anonymously.

*Crafting an effective statement.* We believe these statements are most effective when they give specific examples of IRAs and other forms of oppression that are impossible to discount. For example, someone could list experiences such as "On a daily basis as a woman in this office, men comment on my clothing choices—'Oh, she's wearing a color today, not just serious black!'—or tell me to smile more so I don't look too 'sad' or 'serious.'" Or, "I noticed that the open-use workspace with the best furniture and art happens to be down a few steps, meaning people who can't use steps can't access it."

Effective statements also anticipate and preempt defensiveness by situating these occurrences within a broader context (such as your industry, society, or the world) and inspiring decision makers to pursue change: "I know these are common things that happen in the world and across all workplaces. However, I also know that building a diverse team that feels supported is really important to this company. It aligns with our organizational values to be leaders in this wave." Next, effective statements provide specific suggestions like "I have heard excellent things about the Restorative Justice training program and think it could be really effective in our organization. I also think it would be amazing if the company leadership would read the following books and provide them for all to read." Finally, effective statements validate the difficulty and reinforce why this will be ultimately helpful to the company: "While I know this is going to cost money and time and will bring up difficult emotions, I strongly believe that engaging in this work will reduce turnover within our workforce and foster much more effective and productive teams. We also know from research that maintaining diversity among staff leads to better product output—what do we have to lose?"

Of course, not all attempts at advocating for change will be received well. Those seeking to make change should carefully assess their safety and the potential consequences before doing so. When possible, build coalitions to increase pressure and minimize the risk to any one employee. Seek out trusted members of the organization who share your values but have more leverage and authority to press for change on your and others' behalf. If advocacy is met with rejection or retaliation, consider seeking additional supports from Human Resources, a company ombudsperson, Quality Assurance, or other internal reporting structures. External legal consultation may also be beneficial. If you have the financial security and, perhaps, geographic flexibility to do so, consider leaving the organization. For suggestions on how to sustain yourself, see chapter 12.

# CHAPTER 11

# BUILD THE HORSE
# BEFORE PRESENTING THE CART

· Guillermo's Story ·

Guillermo, a Peruvian American trans* male, walked into the weekly staff meeting with a large iced coffee and prepared to be bored. He picked the chair in the corner farthest from where the boss sits, his intricate doodling hidden from view. Staff meetings always felt like an inefficient use of time. It was the same week after week—fifteen minutes of content predictably ballooned into the requisite sixty-minute block of his life. Guillermo began to calculate the wasted hours in his head. Listening to the boss wind her way through the agenda was sheer drudgery. At 10:35 a.m., though, something startled him into the moment: "Next on the agenda, diversity." He felt a shiver down his spine as he prepared for the multitude of possibilities that could follow. "We don't have enough diversity here and people are commenting on it," his boss continued. "Our staff page is pretty much all Caucasian people." He felt a few eyes look toward him and quickly skirt away. Are people really still saying "Caucasian?" he thought. "Angie," the boss said to another employee, "can you find some diverse stock images to make our website more welcoming to people of color?" Now others chimed in: "Maybe we should do some diversity promotion in our social media or something." "I could look on LinkedIn to find people of color to reach out to offer an interview." "I know!" said John. "Let's plan a party *where we all bring a dish from our culture and talk about what it means to be of Irish descent, or whatever."*

At the next staff meeting, they scrolled through the "new and improved" website and colleagues reported on the number of interviews scheduled with diverse candidates. Guillermo's mind filled with images of people scanning the website, drawn into this place like insects to a Venus fly trap. He pictured their faces, hopeful that the alluring words and images captured on the website were backed with a longstanding commitment to diversity and equity. Guillermo could feel their disillusionment upon learning on day one that he was the only person of color at the company and had been stuck in a low-paying, entry-level position for seven years. He could anticipate the bias incidents and pain that would follow, never to be followed by an acknowledgment or apology. It was frustrating for Guillermo to watch his colleagues grabbing for a diverse workforce because they knew it would reflect positively on the company. Maybe they even knew the company's bottom line would benefit from the move, even without having first done the work necessary to make the environment safe for folks like him.

## WHY THIS IS PROBLEMATIC

In our consulting work we often hear stories very similar to Guillermo's, either from people with lived experiences or from leadership committing the same faux pas. We call it the "cart before the horse" phenomenon, and it is extremely common. Typically the pattern goes something like this: an event within the institution (overt discrimination, an employee complaint) or an outside event (the death of Breonna Taylor, a contentious presidential election) acts as a spark, causing so much raw emotion that members of the organization are compelled to talk about these issues. Incredibly, folks find ways to break through even though they've been socialized to avoid talking about these issues in the workplace, and the conversations, like live wires, ignite even more sparks. Employees and consumers press for change, and in this rapidly escalating chain of events, leadership is concerned that failure to respond effectively will threaten their own reputations or that of the company.

Next, lots of meetings are scheduled. Sometimes these meetings quickly lead to leadership reaching out for external consultation. Other times we see organizations turn inward to ask employees with marginalized identities to sit on panels and join town hall meetings to educate leadership on how to improve things. Typically, after one or two of these meetings, emotions escalate and the desire to end the tension and "fix the problem" intensifies. This is where the cart comes in. Organizations want to be perceived as having arrived at the place where a diverse workforce gets along, functions as a team, and feels mutually empowered.

*The Logistics Magnet.* While leadership is working through their meetings, additional meetings are simultaneously being held in subunits or programs throughout the organization. Staff will begin to share stories about how they personally relate to or interpret the events, which often surfaces even stronger emotions. As feelings intensify, groups become similarly motivated to generate solutions, especially to quell the escalating hurt and conflict. Most staff aren't skilled in or trained to have effective group discussions across differences (intergroup dialogues). These conditions present prime opportunities for being drawn to what we call "the Logistics Magnet." This is when the group shifts its focus from the challenging and often distressing underlying issue to, you guessed it, logistics. The phenomenon is fairly predictable under these conditions and is easy to spot if you know what to look for. It might start with a single suggestion: "Why don't we create a website that looks more diverse and welcoming?" An unconscious but collective sigh of relief moves through the room, as staff have found a way out of feeling the distress—guilt, hopelessness, apathy—associated with their lack of diversity. A related but equally distracting suggestion might follow: "We could have a potluck and ask each employee to bring a dish that represents their culture!" These opportunities allow everyone to find their niche and engage in doing something that feels constructive and comfortable, like web design or event planning. These activities are safe and superficial but create the illusion of progressing toward a meaningful goal. The decision to build a website with diverse images, arrived at during Guillermo's staff meeting, served a dual purpose. Not only did the suggestion deflect attention and feelings away from the underlying (and much more challenging) issue to be resolved, but the new website catapulted the organization hundreds of miles ahead. They didn't pause for even a moment to reflect on *why* their workforce was so homogenous. They didn't take time to learn how to make themselves more safe and inclusive to work with or for people like Guillermo. The Logistics Magnet is enticing because all of the participants appear to win. In this case, the staff are completing their assignments and deliverables, feeling productive and probably enjoying socializing during the potluck. The organization has a splashy new website to show for their efforts. The site not only reflects positively on the organization; it succeeds in attracting more diverse candidates and hires. Somewhere in the organization, a manager is getting credit for having successfully met the new hiring standards. Organizations frequently start building their cart to present to the world, forgetting that it must first be anchored to a strong horse before it can move forward. When this happens, Guillermo and those who unwittingly hop on the unstable cart lose.

Putting the cart before the horse can be dangerous and cause even more heartache than simply maintaining the status quo. Try to imagine being one of few people of color in your workplace and on the receiving end of identity-related aggressions on a weekly or daily basis. Suddenly, your organization starts to drop images of Black and Brown people on its website, in its marketing materials, and throughout its digital video signage. Try to imagine being gender queer, having they/them pronouns, and, yet, your colleagues regularly refer to you as "she." Then you click the link to the new website and see a gender-neutral-appearing person with rainbow lines bordering the image. In both cases, one experience is entirely incongruent with the other. At best, the incongruence is disconcerting and at worst it creates anxiety and disillusionment.

The "cart" is the *image* of doing the work—the cosmetic shell of doing the work—whereas the "horse" is the process of learning about one's own identity and positionality; how that positionality affects and interacts with others; practicing conversations across difference: accepting the gracious gift of feedback; and consistently accessing new resources to self-educate.

## WHAT TO DO ABOUT IT

When building the horse, we encourage you to keep it SIMPLE. The SIMPLE acronym offers a useful framework and litmus test when you're preparing to ignite and sustain a culture shift within your organization. Each of the strategies below adheres to at least one of the SIMPLE principles, which remind us to ensure that efforts will be experienced by all members of the organization as Safe, Informed by data, Multiculturally responsive, Proactive, Leveraged, and Enduring. First and foremost, attending to building the horse before hitching the cart incorporates all six SIMPLE tenets. As you consider the following recommendations, see if you can link them back to elements of the SIMPLE framework.

*A word about safety.* The notion of safety recurs throughout this book. That's because cultural shifts cannot occur unless people feel safe to take risks. Moving against the status quo in all organizations is risky. For example, were the NFL to suddenly decide to promote mental health among players by offering on-site therapy, without first addressing stigma and dispelling common myths about mental illness—such as strong athletes don't deal with anxiety or depression—the mental health programming would have no chance to succeed. There is a principle in group psychotherapy that illustrates this point: "The group members will feel as safe to explore difficult issues as the *least* safe and most vulnerable person in the group." When people with rising identities are recruited into workplaces that aren't skilled and prepared to receive them, IRAs and other oppressive incidents proliferate. And that's not safe. Before hosting dialogues and implementing strategies for promoting inclusiveness, make it a standard practice to ask, "Who are the most vulnerable individuals in this setting at this time under these circumstances and what do they need to feel safe?"

*Reflect on the emotionless workplaces fallacy.* It is commonplace for people advocating for identity-related training or restructuring within organizations to be met with responses like "That's a really tense topic. We don't bring our emotions into the workplace," "Our work with structural engineering has nothing to do with emotions or race," or "If employees are struggling emotionally within our institution, we encourage them to seek out counseling through the Employee Assistance Program or Human Resources." If you are a leader and these statements sound familiar, take heed. If you are white, you have never experienced the sting of racism interwoven throughout the workday. If you are a cisgender man, you have never experienced the recurring pain of being undermined or ignored in meetings as a woman. Just because you haven't had your negative emotions personally evoked in the workplace does not mean such emotions aren't there. Rather, you just might not be able to see them. Stating that "we don't bring our emotions into the workplace" is oppressive. These words erase the heavy, long-standing, and persistent sadness, hurt, anger, and pain endured and suppressed for years by employees with rising identities. The emotions that you claim are "not appropriate for the workplace" are already here. If you have had the privilege of not having to confront identity-triggered emotions in the workplace, bringing them up and addressing them will undoubtedly feel worse at the start. Experiencing and naming increased discomfort by those who hold privilege and power signifies growth. Addressing the issues that evoke the emotional discomfort may be your best opportunity to make things better for colleagues with rising identities. Naming the emotions that have been there all along is a way of showing respect.

*Prereading.* Building the horse might start with requiring the white people within the organization to read articles or books, listen to podcasts, or view videos and other web-based content. Books such as *White Fragility* and *How to Be an Antiracist* have become popular choices for organizations since the heightened racial consciousness of 2020. Starting with required review and processing of multimedia resources allows people to begin the learning process in private, which can be beneficial for multiple reasons. First, offering educational materials on a variety of platforms lowers the barriers to accessing those resources and increases the chance of staff consuming them. Second, this work can be uncomfortable, so it can be more productive to start (or continue) it within the safety of your own home. Under the cloak of privacy, most people will feel safer to express the feelings that would be discouraged in most workplaces. In private, you are free not only to *feel* deep sadness, anger, defensiveness, or shame, but to *act* on those feelings as well. You can cry, slam the book down or hurl it across the room, shut off the computer, complain, express doubt, or disengage. You can weep openly when the words on the page validate the experiences you have had to suppress for years just to function at work. You can set the book down for a minute or a few days while letting the emotions surge and subside, allowing for new tracks of learning to be laid. Reading can also be helpful because it reveals to those of us with privileged identities within the specific identity topic a vast body of knowledge. These educational materials contain important statistics, history, and shared and lived experiences revealing the topic at hand. Within these materials, staff will begin to uncover evidence-based strategies for "what to do about it." Seeking, looking up, accessing, and using these resources is a powerful but often overlooked skill set. In our work we have been struck by the number of times people, including scientists, researchers, and writers, exclaim that they "had no idea that such a wealth of materials even existed." People typically take the easy (and harmful) way out by simply asking colleagues or friends who hold rising identities, "What am I doing wrong? Just tell me! I want you to feel welcomed and included here and that this is a safe place," or "What should we do next? How can we fix this?" Preparatory reading and self-reflection can position the entire team to be more confident and effective when they enter a room together. Taking the time and effort to establish a shared language and knowledge base from which everyone can proceed together can make subsequent intergroup dialogues more likely to move the organization forward.

*Cultivate a shared culture of continued discovery.* Once your organization begins to see the value of prereading, consider developing a shared, virtual library where this ever-expanding body of knowledge can be housed, accessed, and nurtured by staff. This can be as simple as a shared folder on your company's network or any online document-sharing system. Plant the seeds for an evergreen library with materials related to pivotal sociocultural moments impacting your organization and surrounding communities, such as public health crises, protests, elections, and debates. These moments are easy to identify because they are the same issues where identity and difference clash and spark dialogue. When people are talking about race, gender, sexual orientation, or other rising identities on the news, that should signal there's probably a new folder to create in your library. While simple, easy, and free, the evergreen library can have an incredible ripple effect.

First, creating the library communicates to the organization that "We care about these issues and wish to grow together in our knowledge and ability to address them effectively." As with prereading, the library creates a safe space where staff can venture to learn about these pressing and contentious concerns. They can delve into topics at their own pace without fear of being exposed for what they don't know. The library also acknowledges that people have different levels of understanding on a given topic, and it should be designed accordingly, typically by subtopics, and it should be easy to both locate and navigate. Once seeded, the evergreen library should be announced by leadership and well publicized in multiple venues. Seeding the library is only the first step. If you think the job is done, your evergreen library will remain static and die.

Step two creates ownership so that, over time, more people assume responsibility for its growth. Step two is where your community's creativity and innovation take root. Consider establishing a core team with oversight of this process. Team responsibilities can include ongoing solicitation and curation of new pieces for the library from the broader organization. The team might select a "resource of the month" and acknowledge the staff contributor. When sharing this resource, the team might present a slate of five or six specific recommendations for how programs and departments systemwide could integrate the resource into their efforts. The team could survey the organization midmonth to learn about novel practices generated by the community and, again, acknowledge or even reward the exceptional practice. In summary, the goal of step two is straightforward: create multiple, engaging, and rewarding opportunities for staff to mold the materials and resources into the fabric of the institution. When properly cared for, your evergreen library will blossom and become a frequently trafficked place where staff take respite and grow year-round.

*Reflect on why your workforce isn't already diverse.* In addition to the well-documented research on bias in hiring, there are a number of identity-related factors that impact who is most likely to be hired. Below our desks and behind our computer screens there is a network, an interwoven web connected by thin roads and super highways. This is our social network, and it is largely influenced by social class. Each time we attend a new school, make a new friend, or join a new organization, our social network grows. We are taught to grow this network, but some are born with built-in superhighways while others start out alone. For example, some people are born into wealthy, highly connected families who can easily find educational and employment placements for their children. Others are the first in their family to graduate high school or attend college and need to build the roads themselves. For them, gaining access to higher education and employment opportunities can be fraught with barriers and feel random and anxiety-provoking. For those with a powerful social network, the same process can be like jumping on a high-speed train with few worries. Typically, the socioeconomic status a person is born into, or acquires, correlates with their level of connectedness with powerful individuals. Socioeconomic status also correlates with race and ethnicity; thus, workforce leadership tends to be largely white and not as diverse when it comes to socioeconomic background.

Reflect on the ways your organization is linked to this network. Do your board members' kids get an automatic summer internship without sending in an application? Do you have a consistent referral stream from certain universities? Do you have special access and accommodations for "VIPs" who come to your school, hospital, or organization? What are your hiring processes? Where are the racial, economic, gender, and socioeconomic bottlenecks? Are they at the application stage, the interview stage, or the offer stage? Ensure that staff responsible for recruitment and hiring are trained along with other employees to identify unjust policies and practices that serve to maintain the status quo. Help staff to first recognize the inequities that sustain your current network. Motivate them to make changes in their recruitment and hiring practices in order to put a little dynamite into that bottleneck.

*Prepare to communicate skillfully.* Listening and dialoguing effectively are critical parts of building the horse, and both processes require specific, learnable skills. For details on learning to listen, see chapter 8 and consider a related training. Exploring resources from the Program on Intergroup Relations (IGR) at the University of Michigan can also aid in this stage. IGR was founded in 1988 at Michigan as a partnership between the Student Life department and the College of Literature, Science, and the Arts. This social justice education program blends theory and experiential learning about social group identity, social inequality, and intergroup relations. It prepares students and community members to live and work in a diverse world and educates them to make choices that advance equity, justice, and peace. Key methods include experiential exercises, structured facilitation by peers, biographical testimonials designed to build trust and interpersonal connections, small-group and large-group discussions, and journaling/reading activities. The course sessions progress through four stages: addressing structural racism, hot topics, conflicts, and allying. Notably, participants are challenged to move beyond insights to action steps. Publicly available resources can be accessed at the IGR website: https://igr.umich.edu.

While reading about the models shared here and in IGR might seem sufficient, we encourage in-person training and feedback sessions to build these skills more effectively. Ideally, teams would have an on-site coach for the first few dialogues to provide in-the-moment instructions encouraging culture shifts within macro- and micro-moments. For example, it can be hard for white people and men to notice that they are taking up the majority of space in the room, as most were socialized to do. A coach can facilitate by making a statement such as "I wonder if those who have not spoken yet have thoughts on this?" Coaches can open sessions by reminding people of the typical Oppressive Listening traps or behaviors to look out for when engaging in dialogues. During the dialogue, the coach can help the group build skills in identifying these moments by giving a small sign—such as ringing a bell, lifting a finger, or some other signal that the group decides on—to denote a misstep.

Continued dialogues will look different within each organization, but there are a few general strategies we have observed to be more effective than others. First, establish that dialogues will be ongoing, expected, and well structured. Set a cadence that works for your organization and adhere to it. Do not rely solely on calling meetings in response to crises. When dialogue skills are routinely practiced, your employees will be able to utilize them more easily in stressful times. Commit to this work on a continuous basis and show that you're not just engaging in the work in a reactive way. Demonstrate your desire to be proactive by working to build trust in relationships. Expect that there will be many more incidents to come. Build your horse to meet those moments as a mutually empowered team.

*Put your money where your mouth is.* Hire outside expertise or create an internal position dedicated to promoting inclusiveness and facilitating employees' growth and learning about core topics like positionality, power, and privilege; identity-related aggressions; and facilitating intergroup dialogues. It is key to provide your team with ample support while engaging in this often murky and threatening work. The process of building inclusive organizations can be much safer and smoother with the guidance of those with significant experience. Securing the expertise for navigating these waters and approaching these challenging topics is a wise investment. We do not believe it is most effective or right to ask those marginalized within your company to educate others and fight for deep reflection and change, though we frequently observe this. Hiring an external consultant provides your company with the skills to manage the intensity and defensiveness that will be surfaced by these conversations.

If you choose to hire someone from within your organization to hold this role, we recommend making this their sole focus. No matter how skilled a contracted professional (or internal team) is, they will illicit negative feelings from and at times be disliked by staff. Encouraging teams to push beyond their comfort zones can be isolating and alienating. This role means receiving intense, emotional, draining emails or having to attend urgent and unexpected drop-in meetings. When your inbox becomes a virtual war zone, opening it can be scary. The decision to open or close your office door becomes a daily struggle, necessitating an internal check: *Can I really handle* anything *that walks through that door right now?* The individual in this role will be most effective if they do not have to read yet another heart-rending message from the new Black doctor who was called the N-word by a patient while her colleagues stood idly by, then run to the bathroom, then join the team planning next quarter's budget. If someone has to hold dual roles within an organization, both may be compromised. The "day job" will be compromised by the fatigue from the identity-related work. The identity-related work will suffer from recurring internal conflicts, such as whether to remain comfortable or intervene when IRAs occur around the watercooler or in the breakroom: *Would it be horrible if I don't intervene? I'm supposed to be the resident upstander. Can I really take it on right now?* Both roles will suffer for the employee's fear of being passed up for a promotion or being labeled as "too sensitive," "unfocused," or "not a team player."

Be mindful that identity-related trainings on topics such as gender, sexual orientation, citizenship status, and race are more likely to be experienced as helpful by those with privileged identities than by those who have been historically marginalized. As someone who has often pushed to start these conversations in institutions, believing that having the dialogue is always better than not, I (author Lauren) learned this new lesson recently. When providing an introductory discussion on the ADDRESSING framework—a model by Dr. Pamela Hays emphasizing the complexity of cultural influences—with a group of recent college graduates, a man who self-identified as a person of color stated, "While I know this topic is important, I don't like exploring my racial identity in a group of primarily white people." In that moment, he had done just that. He had shared about his experience as a person of color in a largely white space and, in the process, educated me and his white peers. He taught me that attending these conversations in the workplace and other settings and observing white people learning to be better might not feel good as a person of color. Similarly, when I (author Stephanie) participated in and evaluated the merits of a specific SafeZone training aimed at creating more accepting LGBTQIA+ settings, I was struck by the degree of dissatisfaction and discomfort expressed afterward by LGBTQIA+ participants. They detailed how it felt extremely uncomfortable to be asked to share their pronouns when they were the only gender-nonconforming person, and that it was deflating to share their personal narratives to educate others, who then responded with defensiveness. They found it draining. I learned a great deal from friends and colleagues who were willing to share the ways in which the training not only had missed the mark, but had also caused more distress among LGBTQIA+ colleagues.

*Resist the Logistics Magnet!* This one can be lighthearted and fun if you let it be known that the Logistics Magnet is an actual phenomenon. Consider having a bell on the table, or a sign that someone can give when they notice the group drifting toward logistics planning or premature fixing in the midst of identity-related discussions.

It can feel awkward to interrupt the flow of a conversation but soon staff will become more comfortable saying something like, "Sorry to interrupt the flow, but I fear we've been sucked up into the Logistics Magnet vortex!" When folks become more mindful of the Logistics Magnet and more skilled at calling it out, they can progress to more advanced skills. The ability to name and sit with discomfort is one of the most important muscles to develop in becoming a more inclusive organization. At this stage of growth and development, signaling the drift toward the Logistics Magnet could be followed with an understanding of the trigger: "I think we drifted right after Amen shared his experience of feeling unseen in his disability status. I know that I felt really sad and guilty when he said that. Maybe we could sit with that a bit longer? What did others feel?"

# CHAPTER 12

# SUSTAINING YOURSELF

· Stephanie's and Lauren's Stories ·

*The novel coronavirus pandemic was surging in the Northeast by the mid-dle of spring 2020 and Boston had been in full shelter-in-place mode for what already felt like an eternity. Terms like "Zoom burnout," "the new normal," and "maintain safe social distance" were settling into our con-sciousness. I (Stephanie) was shifting my entire mental health program to Zoom and my calendar was more than full, but I was making room for more. Even at this early stage of the virus's progression in the US, there was a steady drumbeat of reports that Black people, Indigenous people, and People of Color (BIPOC) were disproportionately contracting and dying from COVID-19. This should have surprised absolutely no one. It was in line with what we already knew about longstanding disparities in the delivery of health services to those communities, and in the health outcomes as well. Of course I said "yes" to an invitation, and then an-other and another, to address the mental health impact of the pandemic on BIPOC communities. As bleak and staggering as the statistical reports were the personal stories behind the grim numbers. I read about the be-loved young Brooklyn schoolteacher, Rana Zoe Mungin, who was denied COVID-19 testing three times before finally testing positive for the disease and succumbing to the virus. I studied a photograph of Rana, smiling and unsuspecting, in the* Boston Globe *and thought,* She could be my sister Debbie. *And so I said "yes," I'll sit on your panel and town hall* meeting to discuss the impact of COVID-19 and forced relocation on international and BIPOC college students facing food, housing, and Internet insecurity. I said "yes," I will conduct a workshop with your coaches about how to support the little Black and Brown kids who are anxious and grieving about sick and hospitalized family members. I said "yes," I'll consult with your law firm, your sales team, and your bank managers about issues related to coping, surviving, and managing in the pandemic. Deep down, I was feeling it was already too much, but I couldn't bring myself to set limits, certainly not yet; it was, after all, the very life and survival of my community I was fighting for. So, "yes," I'll deliver a training for your workforce on white allying. And isn't May National Mental Health Awareness Month? "Yes," "yes," and "yes" again. "Yes," I'll facilitate a Zoom workshop with BIPOC eleventh- and twelfth-graders; I love working with young people. "Yes," I'll appear on your panel, speak with your membership, answer your questions. This was my expanded "new normal" portfolio. But as May was winding down I was especially excited to be joining a panel with three remarkable Black women psychologists and psychiatrists to discuss the mental health impact of COVID-19 on African American communities. This rare assemblage was for one of Colormagazine.com's signature events focused on empowering professionals of color. Wanting to be well rested and feel prepared for the panel, I turned in early. Although I had been practicing physical distancing from the media, a self-care technique I planned to recommend the following day, I switched to the news just before shutting it all down. That's when I saw it. There was no warning. No trigger message. No disclaimer or advice to look away. There was George Floyd, pleading and begging for his life, to no avail, as a Minneapolis police officer knelt on his neck for minutes on end. I didn't have to see it twice. I didn't need to have it confirmed by another news station. I knew the drill. The video footage was disturbing yet familiar. I switched off the TV, prayed for his family, turned over in bed, and wept.

As a white person, I, (Lauren) felt overwhelmed in the aftermath of Mr. Floyd's killing. I wasn't surprised that it had happened; I was surprised *that it triggered something—that it seemed to be finally hitting people that racism was alive and well. Stephanie and I were being called, emailed, texted, and asked to give talks on "anything related to diversity, really." Everyone wanted to do something, or feel like they were doing something, contributing to the new awakening. We hadn't predicted it, so our calendars were already choked full with other projects. The spreading consciousness we long hoped for was reflected in the flash flood of requests for talks, TV interviews, and podcast appearances. Yet there was no time. There was no time to pause, to feel, to process, and eventually it became impossible to say "yes" to everything. I remember feeling extremely anxious, frustrated, and at a breaking point. I knew that the stress I was feeling—just call it burnout—was nothing compared to the racial trauma that BIPOC people were faced with. Because of that knowledge, I had a hard time saying "no" and setting limits. As a white person I didn't feel like I should take any time to engage in self-care, but not setting boundaries started to show. I started missing important emails. I was checked out during a talk. I responded emotionally to an email chain where leadership exposed themselves as still not getting it, their text revealing every aspect of Oppressive Listening. I felt more angry than inspired by people suddenly wanting to invest in this movement. Why had it taken so long? Why today and not last week? Mindful of not wanting to add further burden to trusted BIPOC friends in my life, I scheduled a phone call with another white person, expressed these feelings, and talked through the workshop and speaking opportunities on the table, prioritizing ones that felt most value-driven and most likely to lead to ongoing change. While it even feels self-centered to write, I feel that setting these limits and taking time to go on a run or nature walk were key to being able to continue with this work. It gave me space to feel gratitude for the movement, engaged and inspired.*

## WHY THIS IS A PROBLEM

Giant mission, little power. Historically, the mammoth task of dismantling systemic, institutional, and interpersonal oppression has been bravely shouldered by a relative few. Many of these (persistent) change agents are themselves actively oppressed and possess little power within the systems they are working to shift. If you are engaging in this work as someone with rising identities, we realize that merely existing in this society can be exhausting. Committing to press for systemic change can be profoundly exhausting. If you engage with this work as a cisgender white man without any historically marginalized identities, we recognize that this work can be draining for you, too.

*Isolating and challenging.* It can be hard to build and maintain relationships at work if you are the colleague who always raises the topics people don't like discussing, corrects people when they use the wrong pronouns, and calls out racist jokes. Colleagues often respond by taking their defensiveness and turning it on the activist or ally, thinking, *This discomfort must be because they are annoying, oversensitive, and whiny.* It can be lonely and isolating, and likely it's not just happening at work; it happens with family and close friends, too.

*Hyperawareness of pain.* Engaging in this work with rising identities means that, when targeted, you do not have the "luxury" of suppressing your awareness of identity-related aggressions, and oppression and related emotions. Instead, you become hyperaware of your own oppression and ever more vigilant of others being oppressed around you. You have taken the *Matrix* pill, and once you start to see the harmful systems that exist, it feels unjust to shut down and stop caring. Once you see it, you can't go back.

*This work can be slow.* As humans we are motivated by rewards. Societal change often happens at a glacial pace, momentarily sped up by traumatic inflection points like the killing of George Floyd. It is rare for "positive events" to expedite change in the same way. These realities can make it difficult to endure the marathon. Thus, we believe that a vital part of trying to create a more just and equitable world is to engage skills to sustain yourself. You are a committed agent of change and we need you to be energized, rested, and healthy. And, to paraphrase a common sentiment, "If you hold a rising identity, your very existence is an act of resistance."

## WHAT TO DO ABOUT IT

*Check in with your values.* Do you value being open and expressive of how you're feeling and what you're thinking? Do you find it hard to suppress your daily experiences (for instance, enduring an anti-Semitic supervisor) for the sake of maintaining your job? Do you feel safe beginning to express opinions and experiences at your workplace? Do you value social justice? If so, do you have enough power within your institution to start to call for it? If you answered "yes" to even a few of these questions, then it is probably a good time to engage with this work. If you answered mainly "no," consider how you can build a support system within your organization to prepare you for future engagement. Ask if you see yourself remaining with the organization for five or ten years and whether you feel motivated to build a workplace worth working for. Remember that while it is important to make workplaces better for those who will come after you, your well-being also matters right now. You can leave the organization with things left undone and unsaid. Understanding your values, and choosing which ones to focus on primarily, can help you pace yourself in a sustainable way, protecting you from developing symptoms of burnout and depression.

*Seek compensation.* Don't hesitate to negotiate for professional compensation for assuming this additional responsibility. Effective DEI work is just as critical to your organization's bottom line as is a balanced budget or a successful advertising campaign. Remind leadership of the powerful messaging sent by valuing this work. The organization's transparent investment and appropriate resource allocation for its stated priorities models best practices and sends a clear message of commitment to those within and outside of your organization. Professional compensation can come in the form of an increased salary or a temporary differential; funding for professional development; a title that includes a budget and decision-making authority; a reduced course, patient, client, or committee load; and awarding of promotional criteria. You might offer additional time off that requires employees engage in social justice activism or positive community change (note that this work should be optional to BIPOC employees or others with rising identities who may find it triggering). Remember that advocating for these resources is not a self-serving proposition. Your efforts to formalize and institutionalize DEI work will benefit the organization long after you and your expertise have departed. Plus, it can feel a whole lot better to do difficult work when you're being recognized and compensated for it.

*Share your talents beyond your workplace.* An effective strategy for sustaining yourself when feeling unseen, unheard, and unappreciated in your department is to actively seek opportunities to perform your work before a broader, perhaps more affirming, audience (a coalition for racial justice or LGBTQIA+ rights, for example, or a community event). Platforms outside of the immediate environment in which you are being marginalized can provide additional sources of feedback, validation, and encouragement. The replenishing, encouraging power of an audience nodding, snapping, and cheering you on cannot be underestimated. The experience of validating others while also validating yourself builds community and provides vital energy to you to continue pressing on. Having people approach you after your presentation to ask questions or share stories can push your learning further and reinspire you to stay engaged. When word of your excellence gets back to your department, colleagues and supervisors alike may take notice and reevaluate their oppressive behaviors and offer you a higher platform to do your work. Even if your team does not recognize your work, you will have expanded your own network and future opportunities.

*Look for others with similar values within the organization.* Have you heard other people talk about experiences similar to yours, whether they share your identities or not? Perhaps you have seen people display symbols of rising identities, such as rainbows, flags of other countries, or religious symbols. Do any of them seem like people with whom you might develop a community that understands what it feels like to be marginalized within your organization or the greater society? Set aside time to speak with these people. Create a coffee break group for meetings (perhaps not outwardly advertised) where people can casually and openly express their feelings and share stories of recent identity-related aggressions at work. Practice building your own skills when speaking to individuals who hold different identities. Building your skills can feel empowering when working within an organization that might not be fully supportive of you.

If you don't have individuals within your organization whom you can trust, make time to engage with people who share identities with you and who will fully validate your experiences. Find a buddy you can call during your commute, vent to via text in the middle of the day, or meet for dinner midweek to make it through to the weekend. If you are partnered, there's a chance that your partner might not be able to be this person for you, or might need to do their own work before being able to support you in this way.

*Be mindful.* "Leaning in" to advance your organization's DEI efforts will have extraordinary professional and personal benefits and costs. Ultimately, only you can determine whether the equation works for you at this time in your career and life. What feels balanced early in your career may become too much of a burden as you advance professionally. Conversely, the stakes may be too high to accept this torch as a young professional who is still learning to navigate the organizational culture and political landmines.

*Celebrate yourself.* As discussed earlier, you cannot expect others to celebrate you when you engage in this work. Ideally they will someday, but it is not likely initially if you are pressing against a stubborn system. If you hold privilege, do not expect those with rising identities to celebrate you. Thus, celebrating yourself can keep you in the marathon. Make a list of new thoughts and realizations you've had in your internal development. Journal about your commitment to change and actions you have taken to make things better. Write about victories you have had, big and small. Validate yourself for the hard and important work you are doing.

*Celebrate others.* Simply acknowledging the presence of those who are underrepresented in your organization can go a long way toward lifting morale, both yours and theirs. One of the most vivid and enduring examples of the impact of being seen is what I (author Stephanie) experienced as a Black undergrad matriculating on the predominantly white campus of Duke University in the late 1970s and early '80s. As I made my way across West campus, feeling conspicuous and homesick for my native Philadelphia, I began to hear my name. It took me a little while to figure out what was happening. It began with nods, smiles, and waves and grew into shouts from across the quad. Over the weeks, loud and buoyant greetings of "good morning" and "hey girl!" became customary. The older Black students at Duke were openly and lovingly celebrating the presence on campus of me and other younger Black students. Their behavior helped us to claim our space in that environment, and their warmth and pride sustained me through many IRAs and remain with me to this day. I strive to pay it forward in the spaces I occupy and encourage others to do the same.

*Engage in self-care.* The importance of self-care cannot be overstated. Taking the time to make a list of activities that give you energy and help you clear your mind or regulate your emotions is time well spent. When downtrodden and fatigued, it's hard to find the motivation to take care of ourselves, let alone generate creative ideas about what we can do to feel better. It is helpful to cope in advance by making this list when you are feeling good. Construct a 2-by-3 grid of self-care strategies. Label the top columns "Things I can do alone" and "Things I can do with others." Label the side rows "Small things," "Medium things," and "Big things." Next, start filling in the squares. Include small things like make a cup of your favorite tea, read your list of things that went well in this work, and step outside and take three deep breaths. In the "Medium things" category: take a thirty-minute bath with aromatherapy, watch thirty minutes of junk TV, and go on a walk or run. In the "Big things" category: spend a day in nature, plan a trip—even if it's far in the future, buy yourself a gift as if it's your birthday, sign up for a class to learn a new hobby or practice an old one. The things you can do with others might include the following: call a friend to vent, send a supportive text cheering someone else on, go on a date, plan a trip with someone, or ask someone to plan a dinner with you where you can just show up. Give yourself permission to take days off. Plan these days off in advance so you know they are there to catch you; a time when you can plan to feel and process your emotions or just step away from it all.

*Find support.* It is important to identify and access support that is internal and external to your organization. This support can take many forms, but at a minimum it should include allies who are familiar with the challenges of engaging in this work. If you're often the one doing the training, it can be restorative to register for a training led by someone else. It can feel grounding and validating to read literature published on topics related to identity, justice, and oppression. If you cannot identify internal supports, ask for them. Ask to be sent to a conference designed to empower those with rising identities. Ask for an internal or external mentor to support your work. Ask for resources to be directed toward your efforts. Ask for external consultation. There are excellent nonprofit organizations through which larger communities of support can be accessed: Color of Change, Project South, and Organization for Black Struggle to name a few. Showing Up for Racial Justice is an organization for white people seeking to end racism.

*Know that it is okay to leave or not act.* Be wary of the "if not you, then who?" message from both leadership and mentees. Just because you can take action does not mean you have to. Just because others may be reluctant or afraid to engage in this risky work does not mean you have to. Remember that your advocacy and talents are benefitting your entire organization—you just being there is a benefit to all. You can choose when to act and when not to. If your workplace is unhealthy and harmful, you do not have to stick around or invest in fixing it. It is completely fine to move on. If you have the opportunity to work with a more supportive team, it is okay to choose that. If you

feel the urge to do something before you go, consider an exit interview or a letter to express your experiences and recommendations for
a call to action.

*Resist enabling.* If you decide to stay, recognize the ways in which staying is enabling the system to remain unjust. Companies will no doubt
brag that they have you, a VP woman of color or a manager who is
an out gay man, onboard. Remaining in an organization in silence
can create an illusion, leading leadership to think, *We must be doing
pretty well. We've had a leader of color for the past fifteen years!* Find safe
ways to signal one-on-one, in meetings with your supervisor or the
company's top executives, that things are not okay and that there is
still work to be done. You can hold your head up high, committed to
excelling at your job, and choose not to remain silent.

Finally, reassess all of the above (and recalibrate if necessary) at
least once every six months and schedule time for this process just as
you would for a performance review or required continuing education. Over time, you should expect to thrive, not merely survive, in
any professional environment. If your organization's trajectory toward
inclusiveness isn't advancing, know when to say "when."

# CHAPTER 13

# ANTI-RACISM IN THE WORKPLACE

### · Jen's, Jonathan's, and Dr. Robierto's Stories ·

*In the midst of the coronavirus pandemic in 2020, the Ivy League elected to make standardized test scores, such as the SAT, optional for all students applying to college. This was great news for applicants across the globe. However, there was a catch: the use of scores would still be upheld for student-athletes alone. It was baffling. These tests have long been regarded as racially and socioeconomically biased, better reflecting family income than predicting future success. Inarguably, by requiring student athletes to submit their scores, those applicants with rising identities would be disproportionately and negatively impacted. The National Association of Basketball Coaches (NABC) called "foul."*

Jen, a fifty-five-year-old Asian American engineering director at one of the world's leading tech companies, was standing in the hallway with Kate, a white twenty-five-year-old manager, preparing to give a workshop on using technology to create zero-energy housing in low-income neighborhoods. Two minutes before the scheduled start time, the coordinator rushed up to Kate, turning her body away from Jen. "We are having trouble with the audio—would you prefer to hold a microphone or are you comfortable projecting?" Kate responded, "Huh? I'm not sure why you assumed I was the leader. Here, let me introduce you to Jen, our incredible tech director."

▪ ▪ ▪ ▪ ▪ ▪ ▪ ▪

*Jonathan, a white director at a nationally recognized art museum, was reflecting on the museum's recent interviews for a new archivist. He was describing how much he liked Tammy, a Black woman, stating, "Tammy was amazing, she's so . . . articulate! I'd like to offer her the job." Marc responded swiftly: "I really liked Tammy, too, but let's be careful not to call her 'articulate,' as that's a common descriptor that white people have used to express their surprise about a Black person sounding intelligent. I'm wondering why that word came to mind for you?"*

*Dr. Robierto, a Latinx resident doctor of color, and his supervisor entered a patient's room to conduct a neuropsych consult. When they entered the room, the staff member who was there looked at Dr. Robierto and in an agitated voice said, "You're here too early! I requested a patient transport after lunch. This patient is about to have an individual consult with the neuropsychiatrist. You people always come too early or too late." Dr. Robierto took a deep breath, thinking this again. He looked over at his supervisor and . . . nothing. After a pause, Dr. Robierto introduced himself and said, "Well, I'm Dr. Robierto and I'm here to conduct the neuropsych consult," and proceeded with the evaluation. There was no apology either then or later. When Dr. Robierto and his supervisor walked back to the office together, the supervisor didn't mention it. It was like nothing had happened.*

### WHY THIS IS A PROBLEM

*Defining anti-racism.* Before we go any further, let's define what anti-racism is, and what it isn't. For so long we have defined people as either "racist" or "not racist." These terms often elicit debate and strong feelings, as the definition of "racist" can vary so greatly. Some people understand "racist" to mean a person who actively, consciously dislikes BIPOC people and engages in overt, intentional acts to hurt them either directly (such as calling someone the N-word), systemically (finding ways to suppress access to voting), or both. Others are taught that all white people are racist, as they are socialized to hold racist beliefs and stereotypes, and if they think racism is bad, they need to actively work against that socialized learning on a consistent basis. The labels of racist and not racist are problematic not only because the definitions vary greatly based on who you are speaking to, but also because they seem static, all-or-nothing, good versus bad.

Recently, the use of the term "anti-racist" has been growing in popularity and acceptance. The Smithsonian Museum of African American History and Culture offers this definition: "Being antiracist results from a conscious decision to make frequent, consistent, equitable choices daily. These choices require ongoing self-awareness and self-reflection as we move through life. In the absence of making antiracist choices, we (un)consciously uphold aspects of white supremacy and unequal institutions in society."[1] We are challenged to move away from global labels and instead take a close look at our individual behaviors and ask: "In that moment, did I act in an anti-racist way?" and if the answer is no, then it was a racist action. Dr. Ibram X. Kendi argues there is no such thing as being "nonracist." He encourages us to remember that "Being racist or antiracist is not about who you *are*; it is about what you *do*." Thus, an anti-racist is also regarded as one who is supporting an anti-racist policy through their actions or expressing an anti-racist idea. A racist is one who is supporting a racist policy through their actions or *inaction* or expressing a racist idea. In any specific moment, our behavior can be construed as racist or anti-racist, changing from situation to situation, meeting to meeting, and day to day.

Returning to our examples above, the NABC coaches were acting as "anti-racists" in calling out the proposed inequitable policy and advocating for student-athletes who would be disproportionately harmed. If those same coaches had known about the test score policy and remained silent, their behaviors would have been defined as "racist." More than likely, some coaches were silent throughout the debate, acting as racists while the larger group took anti-racist action. By highlighting the workshop coordinator's assumption and redirecting her to Jen, Kate was acting as an anti-racist. If Kate had just answered the question in the hurried and distracted moment—"a microphone is fine, thanks"—she would have been acting as racist. Had Marc let the "She's so . . . articulate" moment pass, skipping the potential awkwardness and tension, his inaction would have landed him in the realm of racism.

In short, the anti-racism model focuses on behaviors, as opposed to fueling the idea that there are bad racist people and good nonracist people. Seeing ourselves as either acting to create a more just world or being complicit with the status quo from moment to moment makes this work more malleable, effective, and a little less threatening. No longer can we pat ourselves on the back and say, "I'm definitely not a racist like my Uncle Mike." Instead, we can challenge ourselves to ask in each moment: "Is a racist system or stereotype being upheld? And if so, am I willing to act as an anti-racist in this moment?" If yes, Godspeed! If no, why not?

*Choosing not to act anti-racist.* We might decide not to act anti-racist in a given moment for a number of reasons. We may fear losing a relationship or our standing at work, or shy away from causing conflict. By not acting anti-racist in one moment, an individual may be better positioned to act in an anti-racist way in the future. For example, an Indian American woman might opt to not act anti-racist (in her inaction) today for the sake of swimming in the stream long enough to build power within the organization and act anti-racist later. However, if we choose not to act, we must do so with insight and intention. Name the behavior to ourselves and perhaps to others—we are banking on being able to make long-term change at the expense of hurting people in the present by maintaining unjust systems. We must be honest with ourselves and try to hold ourselves accountable for both our actions and our inaction. From moment to moment we need to make an internal check: "Am I choosing not to act anti-racist because I am fearful of potential personal loss or discomfort?" When choosing not to act anti-racist out of fear, we must try to push ourselves into anti-racist action instead—especially those of us who are white.

*Creating workplaces where BIPOC people can thrive, not merely survive.* In addition to the skills and strategies shared throughout this book, there are a number of specific considerations that we would like to share regarding race. As Mary-Frances Winters wrote in her book *Black Fatigue*, "I have been concerned for some time that the modern-day diversity movement, especially in corporate America, obfuscates racial issues that are unique to Black people."[2] Winters, who is a diversity trainer, adds, "So often, I have been cautioned not to focus too much on race in diversity sessions. Of all the popular diversity topics (age, sex, gender identity, disability), white people, by and large, are most uncomfortable talking about race—especially Black people. It may be because of internalized white guilt. My hope is that, as a result of the new racial justice movement, the corporate world will no longer minimize the issues of Black people." We want to counter the unfortunate practice of avoiding the topic of race by focusing on it here, in this chapter. We believe it is an anti-racist action to use this platform, this privilege, to pause and talk about race, specifically sharing our expertise related to Black and African American experiences.

*Working while Black, Indigenous, or a Person of Color.* When BIPOC employees are hired or invited into predominantly white spaces, there is an unwritten rule, linked to a series of rewards in place to encourage the goal: seem as white as possible. In addition to many survival superpowers, BIPOC employees have the ability to code-switch based on who is in the room. code-switching refers to sets of behaviors that BIPOC employees can switch between depending upon context and environment. Code-switching can include adjusting things like clothing, hair styles, style of speech, gait, and expression. Code-switching is reinforced because when doing so one is perceived as less "deviant" from the dominant group (that is, white people). BIPOC employees who code-switch are able to gain access to better treatment, job or educational opportunities, quality service, and experience lower rates of other forms of discrimination. Indeed, the practice of scaling down the appearance of one's membership in a marginalized group often brings a wealth of "rewards" such as being more likely to obtain a job,[3] being seen as professional and/or a "leader,"[4] facing less frequent identity-related aggressions, and receiving more frequent promotions.[5,6] Code-switching is a form of swimming in the stream.

Code-switching is draining and can reduce cognitive resources and harm performance.[7] When members of historically marginalized groups work to be perceived as conforming with historically dominant groups, they are more likely to experience burnout and have an increased desire to leave the company.[8] While we understand that many of us have to learn to swim in the stream to be accepted and accrue power within an organization, we want to be clear that this is not an acceptable status quo. People engaging in code-switching are using a short-term survival strategy that has a number of short- and long-term negative consequences.

Code-switching constitutes a three-part loss. First and most important is the loss to the individual of the experience of being one's full self in the workplace, the loss of joy, comfort, and self-actualization. Second is the loss of energy, as code-switching leads to fatigue and burnout from the ongoing monitoring of what you might have the urge to do or say and choosing to suppress and filter. Finally, there's the loss of creative input. If employees cannot bring their full selves to the workplace, they cannot offer their full range of creativity, development, and problem-solving strategies. In other words, innovation is stifled. These three losses taken together will likely lead to a fourth loss—that of the individual deciding to leave the organization, which, perhaps subconsciously, rewards their continued suppression. Indeed, we know that there is a higher turnover rate in leadership positions held by Black people.[9]

## WHAT TO DO ABOUT IT—A STEP-BY-STEP PROCESS

*Scan the safety of your setting.* At this juncture, you may feel motivated to put this book down, call a meeting, and excitedly proclaim that you'd like to create a culture where people can bring their full selves to work! However, it is important to pause and ask: Is that really safe? Before encouraging employees to bring their full selves to work, explore the hurdles and landmines that might meet them if they do. Do people make race-related jokes on a regular basis? If so, this would be a highly unsafe setting for a BIPOC employee to enter into. If racist jokes are commonplace, a call-out culture and zero-tolerance policy should be established, fast. Is your leadership mostly white, while the food and environmental services staff are mostly people of color? If so, new BIPOC leaders are likely to encounter a barrage of experiences like Dr. Robierto, such as being asked when they're next going to empty the trash, or asked where the recycling goes, or looked at suspiciously when they walk into their first board meeting. In all three cases, the messages will be painfully clear: "You are in the wrong place, at the wrong time." Call out moments when people make assumptions and aim for diversity in all levels of your organization (for example, ensure that white people are also part of food service and environmental teams). Don't recruit BIPOC employees because you are hoping for insights into a new target market. This practice is tokenizing and furthers the belief that one BIPOC person can speak to the experience and desires of the vast range of people among the BIPOC spectrum.

*Recognize that the effects of slavery are still upon us.* In America, we had 246 years to associate "Black" with "slave." Following abolition, while the label "slave" may not have formally applied, such things as sharecropping, lynchings, Jim Crow laws, redlining, employment discrimination, segregation, and mass incarceration serve to uphold the inhumane and oppressive condition of slavery. Different labels masking similar systems designed to maintain white supremacy. Beliefs that Black people were inferior were so strongly held that it was considered unsafe for a white person to drink from the same water fountain as or share a bathroom with a Black person, and it was illegal to marry a Black person. It has been fewer than seventy years since we legislated "equal" rights, and we remain far from equal. It's still dangerous for Black people to walk or run outside or to drive. It's dangerous to shop, go birdwatching, or turn into a cul-de-sac inhabited solely by white people. Existing while Black is life-threatening and taxing. According to research, African American people experience higher levels of stress throughout the day and have less recovery while sleeping, leading to a higher allostatic load. Consequently and not surprisingly, Black people have higher rates of the risk factors and medical conditions associated with higher levels of stress. Whenever an epidemic or pandemic sweeps the land, these long-standing racial disparities are magnified, but the truth is they have always been visible for anyone who cared to see. Slavery is not a thing of the past. It's ugly shadow looms over our country, our minds, and our interpersonal dynamics. That shadow doesn't disappear at the threshold of our factories, institutions, and organizations. When we walk into the office, when we interview, hire, and train a new staff member who is Black, we evaluate performance. If you are white, you have the privilege of never needing to think about this looming shadow. This is the definition of white privilege. Remember what Robin DiAngelo, author of *White Fragility*, wrote: "White privilege doesn't mean your life hasn't been hard; it means that your skin color isn't one of the things making it harder."[10]

For an excellent overview of the looming presence of slavery, we highly recommend watching the YouTube lecture titled "The Truth About the Confederacy in the United States." Jefferey Robinson, the ACLU's top racial justice expert, delivers a masterful history lesson and outlines what we can do to learn from the dark history of Confederate symbols and combat systemic racism. Spoiler alert: not only does the shadow of slavery endure, but African American history has been intentionally omitted from US history and schoolbooks so that we cannot even connect the dots. The shadow of slavery endures and there are few things as cruel as denying its existence and believing we're "past that."

*Create opportunities for Black employees to move up the ladder into leadership positions.* We know from the research literature that BIPOC individuals have to navigate the workplace strategically to earn promotions, needing to show greater competence than their white peers.[11] We also know that African American people have an incredible amount of resilience and a strong growth mindset. What better qualities could one ask for in a leader? Recognize that Black employees are working harder than their white peers to achieve the same milestones. Act in an anti-racist way by recognizing and rewarding that work. As Booker T. Washington famously stated, "Success is to be measured not so much by the position that one has reached in life as by the obstacles which [one] has overcome while trying to succeed." Thus, anti-racist workplaces give additional financial and promotion benefits to employees with rising identities to reflect the hidden obstacles that must be overcome to achieve each stage of success.

*Hire Black leaders and be prepared to act with integrity.* Spend the extra money on salary to offer a position to a Black expert in the field. Bringing in talented Black people will not only help your leadership team engage in more effective strategic planning, but you will also have important figures of power for BIPOC employees to look up to. As the civil rights activist Marian Wright Edelman once said, "You can't be what you can't see." If you want your BIPOC employees to climb the ladder and add racial and ethnic diversity to your leadership, make it look possible. Passively waiting for BIPOC leaders to work harder than their white peers before they can advance, in the process contributing to undue risk of burnout, is racist.

Once you hire Black leaders, be aware of the pattern of giving them "glass cliff" assignments. Glass cliff assignments are projects or issues to solve that are risky and carry a higher likelihood of failure.[12] People with rising identities are given disproportionate rates of these traps disguised as opportunities. Glass cliff assignments have mostly been studied in women, who are most likely to be hired as leaders when things are not going well within an organization.[13] This phenomenon can be perplexing, but research on the glass cliff phenomenon in women can lend some insight. Kristin Anderson hypothesizes that glass cliff hires are made because women make good scapegoats, are more expendable, and offer a win-win for the company. If the person succeeds, great; if they fail, the company can be seen as egalitarian and fair, then return to their previous appointing methods (preferring white men). Additionally, researchers have theorized that women hired during company crises are not expected to improve the situation, but rather to serve as nurturing and a good place to put the blame.[14] Finally, some believe women are hired during such times because they lack access to the information that would steer most men away from these career-threatening positions, such as insider advice from a network of high-powered individuals.[15]

*Remember the "firsts."* As your organization becomes more racially diverse, remember the burden that comes with being among the first new Black employees. They not only have to break through racist stereotypes and assumptions, proving their worth, but they also might have the role of being "the first Black person Sherry has ever really gotten to know." Being the first employee with a rising identity—both in the workplace and in the social lives of colleagues—can be awkward and taxing. Further, Black people often feel pressure and responsibility to make things safer for current and future colleagues of color. They often find themselves in the position of advocating for other Black employees, either by being explicitly or implicitly asked, or internally motivated to do so.

*Signal that Black members of the organization are valued.* Listen to and elevate Black voices and ideas. According to author and scholar Dr. Tema Okun, white supremacy culture tends to acknowledge and give credit to the same individuals within organizations. Think about who typically gets recognized within your organization and aim to disrupt this predictable pattern. Put resources and energy toward ideas that Black employees put forward and credit their contributions. Don't disregard or disempower ideas offered by Black employees if they don't seem to serve your needs. Instead, for instance, point out in front of everyone that great idea that Sasha had during the meeting.

Routinely assess how much space Black people are taking up in meetings and invite everyone to take the floor more often: "Is there anyone else who has an idea they'd like to share?" Make sure to not always call on a white employee first when looking for ideas or answers. Assess who external partners and clients are defaulting to in the room. Too many times we (authors Stephanie and Lauren) have been in meetings where people defaulted to addressing Lauren. Stephanie is decades more senior than Lauren and a highly respected leader in the field of psychology, so it's very difficult to believe this pattern is not about race. Lauren would be acting racist if she were excited by the attention and the ability to grow her reputation, accepting the stage to share her ideas and expertise. Lauren acts anti-racist when she goes into meetings looking for this type of behavior. From the start, she works to defer to Stephanie consistently. When the pattern begins, she responds, perhaps subtly at first. Typically with eye contact, Lauren turns her body toward Stephanie and looks at her, modeling that the speaker should do the same. When a question is directed at Lauren, she passes it to Stephanie. While subtle, these actions can be easy to recognize (as evidenced by how awkward they can feel at times) and can signal to the speaker that they need to shift their behavior. Ideally, the speaker will shift, and later reflect on what happened and why. If we have a relationship with the speaker or develop one, Lauren can act anti-racist by addressing the pattern directly in a one-on-one conversation.

If, like Lauren and Stephanie, two people have a relationship with each other, they can make time and have the courage to debrief these meetings together. In our case, Lauren might say, "I noticed that Mary kept making eye contact with and deferring to me in the meeting. It felt very uncomfortable for me and I'm wondering if we can take a few minutes to debrief?" Alternatively, Stephanie might say, "Was it just me or did that feel weird? Can we take a few minutes now or later to discuss what just happened in there?" We have had many of these post-meeting check-ins and they have afforded us the opportunity to release the emotional distress and problem-solve what we might do differently when, inevitably, the meeting dynamic is repeated. Our relationship has grown stronger in the process.

*For white people: Watch out for classic mistakes when it comes to complimenting or celebrating your Black colleagues.* Learn common back-handed compliments that are actually identity-related aggressions.

Examples include "Wow, you're so articulate," "You're really pretty, for a Black woman," "You're so lucky that you have toned arms—Black people always look more muscular, I'm jealous," "You look so exotic. What are you?," "You should confront John; he'd be scared of *you*," "Wow, you speak English so well," and "You're so comfortable to work with. I don't even think of you as Black." Don't ask your Black female colleagues how or why they change their hair "so often," how it's longer than last week, or if you can touch it (for more on this topic, read *You Can't Touch My Hair: And Other Things I Still Have to Explain* by Phoebe Robinson). Call out other white people when you see them engage in these racist behaviors. Take them aside and explain why these are not okay things to do or say. Encourage them to send a simple apology text or email. Hold them accountable to do better.

*Call out any acts of racism directly.* As illustrated in the opening stories, show that you will not shy away from addressing these moments regardless of whether they are brief interactions or systemic and enduring patterns of behavior. If you are someone with power within the organization, it is especially important that you model these behaviors. Everyone is following your lead. Never underestimate the power of an individual act.

Like so many in the financially strapped news media industry, Jeffrey, an African American editor, faced intermittent furloughs in the months after the coronavirus pandemic struck. Timing couldn't have been better when a longtime colleague and friend approached with a lucrative freelance editing job. The assignment was straightforward: read a draft novel and provide feedback on the dialogue; specifically, do the characters sound authentically Black? The manuscript was nearly five hundred pages, and Jeffrey was eager to dive in and expand his editorial portfolio. The novel seemed engaging enough, but his enthusiasm for the project waned just pages in. He called a friend to talk it through, reading some of the dialogue aloud: "Ro, they'd bees a dead man, homie!" That was just a sample. His friend responded by validating that this was insulting and would only serve as increased fodder for the stereotypes of Black people.

Ultimately, Jeffrey declined the job. More than the financial loss, he worried about his relationship with his friend and colleague who offered him the opportunity. He sat down and penned the following message: "Sorry for keeping you hanging. I'm going to pass on the consultation. I appreciated the opportunity and wanted to kick in, as this would have been new ground for me. But I've been uncomfortable from the start. I only sat with that feeling this morning. I kept coming back to that unintelligible line above. 'Ro, they'd bees a dead man, homie!' I read it over and over again. I don't know anybody who talks like that. If the author thinks white readers will understand that, or accept that that's how Black people talk to each other, there isn't much I can do. But I won't perpetuate it, or dip into that space for 467 pages. The very notion makes me want to throw up. Sorry. Hope there are no hard feelings."

This solitary act was anti-racist in a number of ways. First, by checking in and valuing his own emotions and health, Jeffrey blocked himself from further racial stress and trauma. He opted out of reading almost five hundred pages of what some white people think Black people sound like and skipped the thread of identity-related aggressions woven throughout. He chose the feelings of Black people over his own enrichment and the financial growth of the author. In doing so, he protected himself and potentially others. In addition to prioritizing himself, Jeffrey also acted as an anti-racist by providing thoughtful feedback on why he was not willing to take the job. Hopefully, this message was seen, heard, received with gratitude, and passed along to the book's author. Ideally, by refusing to take the project, Jeffrey's anti-racist act will catalyze change in the writing, or block it from being added to the literature and from perpetuating stereotypes.

*Name the news.* When another Black person has been killed for driving or walking or jogging over the weekend, don't just start your Monday morning meeting or class as if it didn't happen. Name that it has been a difficult weekend, that people might be feeling all kinds of emotions, that you are available to support or talk if people would find that helpful. Lead the group in a moment of silence or reflection.

Check in with how the group is doing, not expecting a verbal response in all cases, and ask if anyone has anything they would like to
express or share with the group.

*Offer no-explanation-needed days away.* Sometimes, hearing about another colleague enduring an IRA, or another trans* person of color
being murdered, is just too much. Sometimes an employee of color
might not want to process the events of the weekend in the Monday
morning meeting. Creating a company culture where people can take
no-explanation-needed days away can be helpful. This can also work
against mental health stigma or stigma related to chronic illnesses
and invisible disabilities like multiple sclerosis and cystic fibrosis syn-
drome, in which energy levels vary greatly. All employees can settle
into a culture that honors these days away by not asking their colleagues why they were out. The participation of the whole company
averts attention from employees of color and makes the days away
more accessible.

*Give employees who are Black feedback.* So often we see Black employees being let go or passed over for promotions due to issues in their
work performance that could have been addressed and corrected
with feedback. For example, Maya, the only Black partner in her
firm, shared her observations and unique vantage point from years of
experience in the wealth management industry: "My white partners
like Paula are often nervous to give feedback to Black employees because they don't want to be perceived as racist. My Black mentees and
colleagues are often blindsided by negative evaluations. It's a vicious
and distressing cycle and I feel like I'm the only one who can see it."
There are well-documented factors that could perpetuate this cycle.
For example, Paula might worry that by giving Aliyah corrective or
negative feedback about her performance, Aliyah will think Paula
"hates" her and could shut down. Further, because of racial stereotyping, Paula might fear that her comments will activate the "angry
Black woman/person" she worries is lurking inside of Aliyah, triggering a hostile interaction. Paula might fear losing Aliyah, and thus

keep quiet to maintain her company's diversity. Ultimately, Aliyah is not given the opportunity to learn and improve her work, and likely will not advance at the company. Aliyah could get burned out and leave, or ultimately lose her position.

This pattern is harmful in a number of ways. First, assuming that Aliyah is not expecting to get feedback just like every other employee is insulting and underestimates her intelligence and willingness to learn. Second, believing that Aliyah is going to react with anger, hostility, or other negative emotions is acting from an assumption that Black people don't have the ability to self-regulate. On the contrary, Aliyah may very well be experiencing Black fatigue and the cumulative frustration from thousands of "mosquito bites," or IRAs, while living and working in a racist world. Further, failure to provide critical feedback ignores the capacity of BIPOC employees to be resilient, to self-regulate, and to survive racist and oppressive systems on a daily basis.

*Offer mentoring to BIPOC employees with leaders who share their racial and/or ethnic identities.* Returning to the idea that "You can't be what you can't see," it is important for BIPOC people to see themselves reflected at all levels of the institution. In addition to making upward mobility look possible, mentorship can aid BIPOC employees in developing skills to navigate the organization. These mentoring relationships can be extremely powerful and safe(r)[16] spaces where BIPOC individuals can vocalize experiences both positive (sharing insights on who might be an ally within the organization) and negative (experiences of identity-related aggressions or unsafe people). In these relationships the mentor and mentee can develop a networking superhighway, where the mentor can offer their access to powerful people and positions. This works against the pattern of BIPOC people having less access to power and positionality, which has upheld the unequal distribution of generational wealth for so long. Mentors can also offer ideas of ways they believe change can be made within the organization, provide hope, and use their positionality to take action. In return, they can receive inspiration from seeing young BIPOC employees grow within the organization.

*Be aware of the burden of mentoring that you might be putting on the few leaders of color within your organization.* More than likely, if you were to implement the above suggestion to offer mentoring to BIPOC employees who share their racial and/or ethnic identities, there would be only a handful of mentors available, with some identity matches missing. While we still encourage mentoring (and likely this is already happening behind the scenes), the organization needs to recognize the "blessing and the burden" inherent in the mentor/mentee relationship. A critical factor here is to remember the ecosystem in which the mentoring is being performed. For example, when a BIPOC leader mentors a BIPOC employee within a predominantly white institution, their work may frequently center on race-based trauma occurring in the workplace. These conversations can be intense, distressing, and emotionally charged. Often there is no clear-cut solution to be shared; it's not like demonstrating the proper protocol for administering a spinal tap. In addition, employees who hold other rising identities, such as sexual and gender minorities, will recognize a shared bond and a potential mentor/mentee match with BIPOC leaders with whom their only mutual identity is that of being underrepresented within the organization. In other words, oppressed people will seek out others who can offer guidance on how to manage oppression. Thus, an anti-racist organization would both foster these mentoring relationships *and* provide additional financial compensation and a reduced workload for the mentors. Mentoring or office hours should be built into the mentor's work hours (on the mentor's terms of course), with thirty-minute post-meetings time blocks to self-regulate before reengaging. Mentoring should not be treated as an added responsibility on top of the mentor's main role within the organization.

*Identify and offer external professional networking groups that your employees can be a part of, especially if you have limited racial diversity in your leadership.* In addition to strong networking potential, offering these resources can help you communicate in a concrete and productive way that you realize your organization has limitations. It can also help your employees of color feel seen and valued. There are several long-standing organizations that have provided mentorship, networking connections, and emotional validation and support to BIPOC professionals. The Partnership, originally formed in 1987 to promote the advancement of African Americans in corporate Boston, has evolved into an organization that supports multicultural professionals at all levels in an increasingly diverse and global workforce. It has collaborated with three hundred organizations and helped more than four thousand professionals of color reach their full potential in organizations across the country. Professional gatherings such as the "3% Conference" that acknowledge and seek to change the lack of diversity in industries (in this case, the dearth of female creative directors) can be a safe(r) haven for validation, empowerment, inspiration, skill building, and networking. Finding, joining, and supporting such organizations is an excellent way for those with rising identities to sustain themselves. Advertising and paying for opportunities like these are nonracist ways to counterbalance the effects of having a (temporarily) predominantly white organization.

*Model the act of bringing one's full self to work.* Reflect on the ways in which you might not be bringing your full self to the workplace. Then ask what shifts in the company's culture or structure or what events might help you express that part of yourself? This is another excellent time to engage staff directly so that they inform, feel, and own the shift in company culture. Consider reserving Fridays as a day without external meetings. People within the organization can dress in ways that feel comfortable or representative to them without worrying about how external partners might perceive them or the organization. Make it clear that your organization does not uphold racist hair guidelines and you welcome people who may, for instance, choose to wear locs or braids. In your employee manual's dress code, include a statement like the following: "We recognize that historically in the United States visual (or verbal) expressions of ethnicities other than European American have been discouraged or punished in schools, the military, and the workplace. We hope that, eventually, this can be a workplace where people can bring their full selves. Despite this statement, we recognize that employees may not feel safe expressing themselves fully. We would like to make clear that there are no guidelines for hairstyles. Further, we do our best to limit meetings with external clients on Fridays so that employees can dress in a way that feels comfortable to them. Please direct any questions to Dr. Smith."

Have a company party and ask everyone to contribute one song that they enjoy dancing to or find meaningful. You might host a community potluck where everyone brings a dish that is an expression of their ethnic identity, whether it be mofongo or mac and cheese. Yes, white people have ethnicities too—typically European American or Latinx. Have a group meeting where each person brings an item of personal importance and explains what it means. Design activities and projects where people can interact across identities. These dishes, items, and exercises might not always be tied to ethnic or racial identity, but exercises like these can help us practice and model bringing our full selves to the workplace. If we can learn to accept each other's mofongo and mac and cheese with simple appreciation and grace, we exhibit safety and in doing so, encourage another step forward. Note, however, that these "event" efforts will ring hollow or be experienced as offensive unless surrounded by significant training, education, and structural sharing.

Create a company calendar where employees can list holidays or dates that are special to them or an aspect of their identity. For example, in some cultures, celebrating the person's "name day" is more meaningful than their birthday. Send out reminders with cues of how people can acknowledge the person in the course of the workday. Establish a company culture where people practice taking off days that are special or meaningful to them, not just government or Christian holidays.

Create a practice of saying names that are new or have sounds that are not English-centric. From the example earlier in the book, when Dr. Adebayo-Opeyemi first introduced herself, it could be a company norm to ask if a recording of the pronunciation could be sent around to staff to practice. Staff should take it upon themselves to practice pronouncing her name and be ready to use it. This would be an anti-racist practice, in contrast to the common practice of avoiding interaction as much as possible, promising to learn the name next time, or repeatedly mispronouncing the name.

*Commit to consistent efforts to assess and address oppression within the organization.* As Victor Ray stated, "Rather than asking how to bring diversity into the workplace, a better question is why so much power and organizational authority remain in white hands."[17] We recommend all of the above strategies, knowing that the tide is turning and organizations are becoming more diverse. However, it is key to remember that at the end of the day, it is not the responsibility of BIPOC employees to fix the issue of workplaces being historically homogenous. We must engage the strategies above and bear in mind that the issue is a white issue at its heart. The responsibility is on white people to fix the problematic, albeit often subconscious, clinging to power by white hands. White people must honestly reflect and acknowledge that it is more comfortable for them to be led by someone white, who reminds them of themselves. They must honestly acknowledge that it can be scary to imagine more competition for positions or scholarships as we call for equitable hiring and admission policies. Commit to change at the risk of losing some of your own power. By relinquishing power that you may not have fully realized you held, we can eventually all win. Your teams will grow more creative, sustainable, and efficient.

Commitments to these efforts must be consistent, long-standing, and independent from national race-based traumas. So often we see companies and universities reacting to high-profile stories, such as the killings of unarmed Black men and women and gender-nonconforming individuals, with conversations, statements, and actions. However, that energy tends to dissipate after a few weeks or months, leaving the system without resources and bound to return to homeostasis. We ask that you start engaging in the strategies in this book only if you are willing to do so for the long run. Doing so in a stop-start way will only hurt company morale and erode any developing trust. This pattern will make it even harder to build trust the next time. If your attempts at making a more sustainable, diverse organization are not working, hire outside consultants to help. If outside consultants are not working, hire someone to advance these efforts as their full-time job. Creating an anti-racist workplace is key to retaining employees from across the BIPOC spectrum. Sustaining just, equitable and non-racist organizations is a lot like working to lower your cholesterol. You wouldn't change your diet, exercise consistently for six months, and sweat like never before only to reach your target and stop. You have to work every day to stay within a heart-healthy range. Otherwise our cholesterol levels will creep right back into the danger zone. Similarly, without constant cognitive and behavioral effort, our minds will revert to the way they were socialized, to what we know, to what is comfortable and easy. As Dr. Kendi explains, "To be antiracist is a radical choice in the face of history, requiring a radical reorientation of our consciousness."

# CHAPTER 14

# FOLLOW THE DATA TO THE FUTURE

A S INDIVIDUALS AND ORGANIZATIONS STEP INTO THIS WORK it can feel overwhelming, daunting, and at times even titanic. Some members of the leadership team will be all in; others will be committed to indifference or worse. And even with the tools and strategies in this book at the ready, no one-size-fits-all road map will pave the way. No one said building better, stronger, and more resilient organizations would be easy. This is a good time to remember to breathe. It's also a good time for reviewing and collecting data unique to your organization—information that will undergird the specific strategies, skills, and resources discussed throughout this book that you elect to implement. Let the data guide you and help illuminate the path for others.

What kind of data are we talking about? You likely already have at your fingertips information concerning your institution's interviewing and hiring, promotions, compensation and rewards, and basic information about the people who are your users, customers, clients, and patients. We'll talk more in a moment about other kinds of data—the information illuminating your path—that we view as essential. First, an important word about the limits of research data and information—an absence of guideposts you'll have to be cognizant of and account for, or risk seeing your efforts fall flat.

In academia, the research enterprise has been stained by a long and painful history of racially (and otherwise) biased and abusive tools, methods, and practices, a reckoning for which continues, however slowly, to this day. For example, for most of the history of medical and psychological research, Black people were considered to experience less pain than others. Considered subhuman, Black people were routinely and purposely exposed to disease and sterilized, and endured (or died from) exploratory surgeries without anesthesia. Their suffering and overall well-being were of no concern.

More recently, the vast majority of demographic measures used by researchers have been inadequate at measuring most aspects of identity. For example, historically researchers have not asked people if they identify their sex or gender in any way aside from male/female and man/woman. This lack of specificity means that we have almost no data on the ways diseases, psychological disorders, or treatments are different across the LGBTQIA+ communities. Moreover, these actions alienate the LGBTQIA+ community, as there can be no clearer message of "we don't know or care that you exist" than to fill out an intake form and be forced to answer "male/female" when you identify as neither or are not sure if the question is asking about biological sex or gender identity. Research studies modeled after the US Census collect race and ethnicity in inaccurate ways, providing extremely limited information on racial and ethnic differences, and, of course, the vast majority of psychological treatment studies have been performed in white samples.

There is a well-known expression in research that seems especially applicable here: "Junk in=junk out." Information that is riddled with assumptions, woefully incomplete, biased, or simply wrong is an ingredient of a slipshod, ineffectual, and failing strategy, no matter the good intentions. Junk in=junk out, indeed. Working from invalid, inaccurate, and incomplete information can also be dangerous. For example, not asking about sexual orientation limits us from investigating subgroup differences, which makes it impossible to know that a treatment or strategy has harmful effects on those who identify as gay. Thus, it is important to proceed with caution, fully acknowledging the barriers to gathering information regarding sensitive and emotionally charged issues in the workplace. Here, the SIMPLE guidelines, first presented in chapter 11, may be helpful when applied to the processes of collecting and reporting data. Whatever approaches are selected by the organization and our consulting research professionals, ensure that the methods are Safe, Informed by data, Multiculturally responsive, Proactive, Leveraged, and Enduring.

In the aftermath of the killing of George Floyd, researchers are increasingly taking note of abuses and omissions in research methods and calling for change. In June 2020, the journal *Neuropsychopharmacology (NPP)* published a statement on racism, discrimination, and abuse of power in solidarity with several scientific and professional organizations. The statement condemned "any and all systemic racism and racial disparities" and called for "immediate societal attention and policy solutions." Specific efforts emerging from the scientific community include growing recognition that systemic racism represents a public health crisis and lobbying for increased funding to study and address health disparities. NNP committed to "Highlighting journal content that documents the impact of racism on the brain and mental health, and making relevant articles free for all to read and share."[1] This simple act of making research and related data freely accessible to those who might not otherwise have access to it is anti-racist. Making research publicly available also makes it more likely that the findings will not remain in academia but will reach the media and those who need the findings to advocate for justice. Leading social justice experts aptly refer to this field as involving both the "head and the heart." That sentiment has been threaded throughout these chapters. Below, we review types of data that organizations can collect and ways that this process can propel them into the future.

*The head: Collect quantitative data.* Quantitative information is what most people think of when they hear "data"—numbers, averages, frequencies, and other statistics. The data available to organizations can be invaluable, but it's often an untapped resource. To reveal a clearer picture of your organization's social identity profile, assess the rates of individuals with rising identities. Be sure to utilize inclusive demographic forms[2] to ensure you are starting on accurate and affirming footing. Next, investigate retention rates related to those identities: Who stays, for how long, and who leaves? Who advances, and who stays at the same level?

Once you have a quantitative understanding of your company's social identity profile, you can go in a number of directions. Hire an expert to co-create surveys for staff. These surveys might assess employee satisfaction, frequency of identity-related aggressions, the perception of the organization's overall cultural awareness and humility, and related metrics. For example, a survey could ask employees at all levels to rate their personal management, referred to as a self-report, and colleagues' skills related to the topics covered in this book. This could include how skillful staff are at identifying and addressing issues related to identities, initiating and facilitating identity-related conversations, or acknowledging when hot topics are impacting the community. Additionally, employees can list the specific actions they are taking on a daily, weekly, and monthly basis to create a more empowering, less oppressive workplace. Hiring an expert to help design and analyze these surveys can aid in ensuring privacy, accuracy, and meaningful feedback. Taken together, this information establishes a baseline and makes it easier to understand where your company stands. The baseline can be used to set future goals and, importantly, can help you know when these goals have been achieved. Additionally, the results of these reviews and frequency of identity-related conversations can be explicitly linked to performance reviews, bonuses, and promotions. Linking this work to monetary rewards clearly signifies your values, motivates people to engage in hard work, and compensates people for the additional emotional labor they are expending to invest in and advance your organization.

*The heart: Collecting qualitative data involves interviewing members of your organization in a semi-structured way.* A series of open-ended questions are asked, such as, "What's your experience of gender in the workplace?"; "What do you imagine when encouraged to 'bring your full self to work'"; and "What is your experience of race within our organization?" Qualitative interview questions are meant to generate narratives, follow the train of thought of the interviewee, and reveal themes and issues yet to be uncovered. Qualitative interviews assume that the interviewee knows a great deal about the question at hand, so questions should spark longer narrative responses, as opposed to pulling for yes-or-no answers. After interviews are completed, responses are organized into themes across interviewees. Themes might reveal specific problem teams or individuals and identities that are being overtly and/or covertly oppressed within the organization.

Qualitative interviews are helpful in capturing the experiences that exist between the lines that are hard to quantify in numbers. In reviewing narratives from staff throughout the organization, factors contributing to the leaky pipeline can be revealed, burnout contributors and levels assessed, and the ways in which identity is interacting with staff's experience can be better understood. As described in chapter 8, Listening Tours are an effective way to collect qualitative data. When conducting qualitative interviews and/or a Listening Tour, we recommend offering in-person, one-on-one interviews; group interviews and focus groups offered by organizational structure and affinity preferences; and an anonymous written submission platform, as the employee/member's preferred method and perceived safety will vary greatly. More structured assessment can be embedded into Listening Tours as well. For example, listeners, speakers, and observers can be asked to complete brief surveys immediately following each session. These surveys can compare themes spoken and heard; rate perceptions of Empowering versus Oppressive Listening skills; and document next steps that can be taken from the perspective of all three roles.

Organizations might opt to take their data to the next level by hiring an external research consultant to perform a comprehensive needs assessment or climate survey using best practices. These research methods might involve providing employees with questionnaires to assess employees' identities; experiences of support, empowerment, and oppression; the frequency of identity-related aggressions they experience; and possible interventions that could be implemented by the organization. Needs assessments typically include both quantitative and qualitative components.

*Don't rest on your laurels.* There is always work that can be done! Even after decades of engaging in this work, we will all have more to do. This underscores the tenets of Cultural Humility: a commitment to lifelong learning for individuals and the institution. Returning to the contrast between cultural competence and cultural humility, collecting data only following a shocking recent event suggests an endpoint or completed task. Application of the Cultural Humility approach to data collection means incorporating these assessments into your organization's annual schedule, and embedding the process of gathering, reporting, and responding to research findings into the company culture. Finally, as part of the evaluation process, remember to reexamine the infrastructure, including committee topics and structure, leadership, membership, and participation. Different stages of the work will require changes to most of the above, so these groups should not remain static. Don't be afraid to revisit, retire, and reconstruct committees and task forces whose structures are not advancing the cause. Failure to do so can send a negative message to your workforce: "We're going through the motions." Maintaining a static and misaligned infrastructure conveys neglect and apathy, like a website that is seldom or infrequently updated with new information. Leaving a do-nothing infrastructure in place suggests, "Our efforts have stalled" or, even worse, "Our institution lacks the necessary bandwidth or interest to properly resource these efforts." Reexamine, refresh, and reconstitute these committees and structures so that they can continue to carry you into the future.

## THE FUTURE OF WORKPLACES

In this final section, we will share our vision for what we believe the future of workplaces can be when employees and leadership across industries consistently commit to practicing the skills referenced throughout this book. Did you notice that we didn't say "diverse" workforces? Instead of constantly striving for more diverse work-places, it's homogenous ones that will be the anomaly. Future work-places will be filled with diversity across all sociocultural identities. Others won't bat an eye at the new employee who shows up for their first day wheeling into the staff room. They won't be surprised when the new hire for the marketing director position is in her sixties. Pi-oneers will be a thing of the past. In these workplaces diversity will be valued, and we'll seek even more of it because we have seen how much it has enriched both our work and our personal lives.

*Future workplaces will carry anti-racism beyond racism.* Workplaces of the future will apply the "anti-racist versus racist" model to all so-ciocultural identities. We'll come to understand, for example, that we are being heterosexist when we ask the new kid in our class-room what their "mommy and daddy" do for a living. We are being anti-heterosexist when we intervene when a colleague says, "Bisex-ual people are greedy—leave some for the rest of us!" We are being anti-Semitic when we schedule important or required meetings or staff retreats on Yom Kippur. We are being anti-anti-Semitic when we have a sense of the religious affiliation of our employees and load all holidays into our company calendar, being thoughtful to schedule around them. We are acting classist when we only interview appli-cants from prestigious universities. We are acting anti-classist when we intervene when seeing this behavior, stating, "It's likely that there are many incredible, intelligent people who did not have access to schools like Harvard or Princeton. I'd like this to be a company where we appreciate what people can do, not just where they went to school." Employees will engage in consistent self-reflection on when they are acting sexist, ageist, homophobic, racist, ableist, classist, transphobic, or xenophobic, and dare themselves, one another, and the system to act anti to each of those domains.

*Future workplaces will support and properly resource the additional effort and cost of being just.* Future workplaces will recognize the value of investing in the sustainability of those with rising identities and will view these investments as being as important as improving the company's profitability. Being anti-ist (racist, sexist, homophobic, and so on) will mean taking action when you hear of something that could be done to make the system more just. For example, if an employee learns about an anti-ableist policy at a friend's workplace and does not seek to implement such policies and resources at their own organization, they would be acting in a manner that is ableist. Learning that a company has accommodations and supports for people with learning disabilities and ADHD and not bringing the idea to leadership would be acting ableist. Similarly, hearing that a department created a list of restaurants for off-site meetings and events that are convenient and welcoming to people who use wheelchairs and not seeking to replicate the practice would be ableist.

*Identity-related discussions will be approached with bravery and skill.* Company culture will develop to a place where colleagues address identity-related aggressions, big and small, quickly and skillfully. White tears will not claim the stage in the room. Rather, those with rising identities will be the focus and will be validated in their pain and acknowledged for the oppression they have had to endure. To make space for these conversations organizations will offer regular, multipronged resources. They will offer practice in groups and dyads, and offer space for self-reflection. They will offer free copies of books like this, and others written for those with both privileged and rising identities. Workplaces will hold an "it's never too late" stance related to addressing the multitude of identity-related issues that are bound to arise. These practices will give organizations permission to evolve through corrective measures as soon as issues are identified. There will be no shame in calling out or responding to IRAs, and when doing so, coworkers will graciously afford one another time and space to gather their thoughts.

*Organizations will budget for ongoing work to empower their employees.* Throughout this book, we have shared a number of skills that can be employed by both individuals and organizations. In many instances taking these steps will require additional resources. Hiring external consultants or creating internal positions to properly implement these strategies is costly. When evaluating the cost effectiveness of hiring a Diversity, Equity, and Inclusion expert or contracting for identity-related trainings, try not to see them as siloed expenses. We encourage organizations to consider the broader financial impact, which might include the costs of low employee retention, repeated onboarding, loss of productivity due to employees' carrying unnecessary burnout and fatigue, having a reputation as a racist employer or organization, and missing out on myriad benefits of having a diverse staff that works well together. Companies of the future will consider all of these factors in harmony, demonstrating highly profitable and wise investment decisions.

*Require cultural humility.* Future workplaces will make it clear through hiring and managing practices that being a part of this organization means commitment to ongoing self-reflection on positionality, practicing dialogues across difference, and engaging in anti-oppressive actions. Those who continuously oppress others without showing improvement will be excused from the organization to protect its people and its culture. On the other hand, employees who act as anti-racist (or anti-oppression) will be rewarded and given more power within the organization. Demonstrating excellence in the practice of cultural humility will correlate with career advancement and recognition.

*The Future of Your Workplace.* We hope that you can visualize your organization as a setting with the potential to reach the goals depicted above. If you recognize yourself (your thoughts, actions, and feelings) or your organization in any of the scenarios presented throughout the book, we hope you feel empowered to try new approaches. We hope you will return to practice the specific suggestions and exercises and commit to a lifetime of discovery that, with time and sustained effort, overrides years of socialization. We hope that you will trust the process, have faith, and persist. Finally, we hope you will be able to recognize and celebrate success when it appears in the form of people holding both rising and privileged identities relating and working together more effectively. We sincerely hope to meet you in the workplace of the future. We'll bring the mofongo and mac and cheese.

# GLOSSARY AND
# A FEW TIPS TO GO

## GLOSSARY

**ADVOCATES:** Members of one or more rising identity groups (e.g., Black, Indigenous, People of Color) working towards a less oppressive society related to their identity (e.g., advocating for more equitable or just systems related to race).

**ALLIES:** People who hold privilege within an identity (e.g., race being white) fighting for systems and people to be less marginalizing.

**BIPOC:** An acronym for Black, Indigenous, and People of Color, coined to distinguish the experiences of Black and Indigenous people that are different from other people of color due to histories of slavery and colonization.

**IDENTITY-RELATED AGGRESSIONS (IRAS):** A term we coined to remove the "micro" from microaggressions. IRAs refer to conscious or unconscious statements or actions that target someone's rising identity. Examples of IRAs include clutching a purse when a Black person walks by; saying, "You're really pretty for an Asian"; or taking advantage of unearned privileges at work that those with rising identities are not offered. The IRA acronym reminds us of the cumulative effect that these harmful incidents have on targets.

**MYTH OF THE MODEL MINORITY:** This racial stereotype asserts that some groups of color (such as Asian people) are more intelligent and successful than other groups of color (Black and Latinx people). This stereotyped belief allows those in power (white people) to maintain power, as it encourages subgroup comparisons and division, reducing the likelihood of coalition building across groups of color.

**POSITIONALITY**: How one identifies across sociocultural identities. Our positionalities usually include a combination of intersecting privileged and historically marginalized identities. Knowing our own positionality, how others see/perceive us, and how we interact with people who hold other identities is key for understanding our historical role in society and how we can work to improve ourselves and the systems around us.

**PRIVILEGE**: Having one or more sociocultural identities that have historically held power in the country in which you live (for example, being white, male, or cisgender) in the US.

**SOCIOCULTURAL IDENTITIES**: The identities we hold that have historically been associated with oppression, power, and privilege in society. We use an adapted version of Dr. Pamela Hays's ADDRESSING framework (2001) which includes identities such as Age (number of years alive and cohort), Disability (physical and learning), Diagnosis (mental health), Religion, Race, Ethnicity, Socioeconomic status, Sexual orientation, Indigenous heritage, Gender identity, and Gender expression. Exploring one's own identities (and how they interact with the identities of others) across the ADDRESSING framework is a helpful way of learning to understand one's positionality.

**RISING IDENTITIES OR POPULATIONS**: A more empowering term to use instead of such standbys as "minorities" and "marginalized" when talking about groups that have been historically underrepresented or marginalized. Dr. Melanie Tervalon, co-author of the construct and practice of Cultural Humility, coined this term.

**SHADEISM**: Discrimination based on skin color, also known as colorism. Shadeism is a form of prejudice or discrimination in which members of the same race are treated differently based on skin tone, with a marked preference for lighter-skinned people. In addition to the US, many countries across Africa, Asia, and South America have lighter-skin privilege.

**SOCIAL JUSTICE TIME WARP**: The experience of going backward in time, or regressing in terms of social justice perspective and inclusiveness across settings. For example, one might move from an organization that engages in daily discussions about identities to one that has never had a diversity-related assessment or training. The time warp reflects a "behind the (desired) times" status regarding social justice/identity IQ.

**TARGETS**: People experiencing instances of marginalization, discrimination, and IRAs.

**TRANS\***: An inclusive way to refer to the range of identities of people who do not identify as cisgender (assigned the gender at birth that they identify with now).

## A FEW TIPS TO GO

Before you go, we want to leave you with a few words and terms to avoid. To learn more about why, do a quick Google search.

1. Caucasian: Instead, say "white." The term Caucasian dates to the 1700s and was an anthropological term alongside "Negroid" and "Mongoloid"; all three are outdated. Further, the term is linked to the belief that white-skinned people are the most beautiful and that the Caucasus mountains were the birthplace of humankind. The related assumption that white people possess the ideal physical appearance is racist.

2. Oriental: Instead, say "East Asian" or use more specific descriptors.

3. Avoid ableist language like "lame."

4. Ways to use (and ways not to use) the word "ethnic": Avoid saying "ethnic" to refer to anyone that isn't white or food that isn't associated with European American/American culture. All people have ethnicities, not just people of color.

5. Avoid saying "I don't see race/color," because let's face it, you do. Saying you don't invalidates the oppression experienced by people who identify as Black, Indigenous, or People of Color.

6. Don't appropriate African American Vernacular English (AAVE) by using terms like "woke" and/or Black gay/queer culture by saying things such as "Yas Queen."

7. Avoid Native identity-related aggressions such as "I'm the lowest on the totem pole" and "let's have a powwow."

8. Don't say, "Your English is so good" or "Wow, I can't even hear your accent." These phrases are hurtful for myriad reasons. First, they assume that someone who immigrated to the US or who does not look white would not speak English well. Second, these statements can be prevalent within non-native-speaking communities, perpetuated by white supremacy, as when an adult who is Latinx compliments a Latinx teen for having a minimal accent. Further, some US immigrants may be fluent in English because their country was colonized by English-speaking people.

9. Don't speak louder, slower, or with limited vocabulary to those whose second language is English, or to people who are deaf or hard of hearing unless you have been instructed to do so.

10. Don't say, "That's so gay," "That's retarded," or "What are you, deaf?!"

11. Relatedly, don't say, "You don't look gay," "He's cute for a guy in a wheelchair," "I couldn't tell you were Black," or "You don't sound Black."

12. Don't tell women to "smile" more.

# ACKNOWLEDGMENTS

F IRST AND FOREMOST, WE WOULD LIKE TO THANK OUR publisher, Beacon Press, and our editor, Gayatri Patnaik, for offering us this platform to share our experiences, opinions, and recommendations. We would also like to thank our family and friends who brought us snacks, read our drafts, and supported us to the finish line. We are grateful to Seth Towns, Roxanne Nesbitt, Chris, and the de-identified voices who shared their important narratives with us. We thank those who built the foundation of our learning on this subject (Stephanie: my ancestors and the Division of Student Affairs at the University of Michigan, Ann Arbor; Lauren: the Clinical Psychology program at the University of Massachusetts Boston and my friends with rising identities). Finally, a special shout-out to our partner, Herb J. Pinder . . . yes, we will send your 20 percent someday. We couldn't have done this without you.

# NOTES

AUTHORS' NOTE

1. Pamela A. Hays, *Addressing Cultural Complexities in Practice: A Framework for Clinicians and Counselors* (Washington, DC: American Psychological Association, 2001).

CHAPTER 1: INCLUSIVE TEAMS ARE BETTER TEAMS

1. K. W. Phillips, "How Diversity Works," *Scientific American* 311, no. 4 (2014): 42–47, doi:10.1038/scientificamerican1014-42.

2. Dr. Melanie Tervalon, the co-developer of cultural humility practice, proposed the term "rising identities" in place of "marginalized." We first learned the term when Stephanie (author) attended a cultural humility training, the last facilitated by Dr. Tervalon, in 2019.

CHAPTER 2: WHAT'S IN A NAME?

1. Joseph P. Williams, "Why America Needs More Black Doctors," *US News and World Report*, August 31, 2018, https://www.usnews.com/news/healthiest-communities/articles/2018-08-31/why-america-needs-more-black-doctors.

2. US Census Bureau QuickFacts, July 2019, https://www.census.gov/quickfacts/fact/table/US/PST045219.

3. Association of American Medical Colleges, "Diversity in the Physician Workforce: Facts & Figures 2006," https://www.aamc.org/system/files/reports/1/diversityinthephysicianworkforce-factsandfigures2006.pdf.

4. B. Bettina et al., "Mentoring Programs for Underrepresented Minority Faculty in Academic Medical Centers: A Systematic Review of the Literature," *Academic Medicine* 88, no. 4 (April 2013): 541–49, https://journals.lww.com/academicmedicine/FullText/2013/04000/Mentoring_Programs_for_Underrepresented_Minority.28.aspx.

5. K. R. Page, L. Castillo-Page, and S. M. Wright, "Faculty Diversity Programs in U.S. Medical Schools and Characteristics Associated with

Higher Faculty Diversity," *Academic Medicine* 86, no. 10 (October 2011): 1221–28, https://www.ncbi.nlm.nih.gov/pmc/articles/PMC3184185.

6. Try noticing all categories from Pamela Hays's ADDRESSING framework: Age, Disability, Diagnosis (mental health), Religion, Race, Ethnicity, Sexual orientation, Socioeconomic status (financial resources/access), Indigenous heritage, Nation of origin/citizenship status, Gender identity, and Gender expression.

7. Evolving from the phrase "cultural competence," cultural humility is a learning goal for people aiming to increase their abilities to work across differences. Cultural humility acknowledges that understanding our own positionality (how we identify) and how that limits our inherent knowledge of other identities is key. Aiming for cultural humility is to aim to build your skills while knowing that this is a lifelong, ever-evolving process, and that we are never deemed "done" or "competent."

## CHAPTER 3: "PIONEERISM"

1. "Pioneer," Free Dictionary, https://www.thefreedictionary.com/pioneered.

2. L. Torres, M. W. Driscoll, and A. L. Burrow, "Racial Microaggressions and Psychological Functioning Among Highly Achieving African-Americans: A Mixed-Methods Approach," *Journal of Social and Clinical Psychology* 29, no. 10 (2010): 1074 99.

3. D. W. Hollingsworth et al., "Experiencing Racial Microaggressions Influences Suicide Ideation Through Perceived Burdensomeness in African Americans," *Journal of Counseling Psychology* 64, no. 1 (2017): 104–11, https://doi.org/10.1037/cou0000177.

4. A. G. Greenwald, M. R. Banaji, and B. A. Nosek, "Statistically Small Effects of the Implicit Association Test Can Have Societally Large Effects," *Journal of Personality and Social Psychology* 108, no. 4 (2015): 553–61.

## CHAPTER 4: BECOMING "EXPERTS"

1. The University of Michigan's Human Sexuality Office was the first staff office for queer students in an institution of higher education in the United States.

2. "Ableism" is a term used to describe discrimination or injustice targeted at people perceived to have disabilities/different abilities.

3. University of Michigan, "About Trotter Multicultural Center," https://trotter.umich.edu/about.

## CHAPTER 5: THIS WORK IS NOT LINEAR

1. Ijeoma Oluo, *So You Want to Talk About Race* (New York: Seal Press, 2018).

CHAPTER 7: WHEN YOU'VE MESSED UP

1. Lee & Low Books, "Where Is the Diversity in Publishing? The 2015 Diversity Baseline Survey Results," January 26, 2016, https://blog.leeandlow.com/2016/01/26/where-is-the-diversity-in-publishing-the-2015-diversity-baseline-survey-results.

2. "Statement from Barnes & Noble," Twitter, February 5, 2020, https://twitter.com/BNBuzz/status/1225120163692937218/photo/1.

3. Mary-Frances Winters, *Black Fatigue: How Racism Erodes the Mind, Body, and Spirit* (New York: Berrett-Koehler, 2020).

4. Roxane Gay, Twitter, January 22, 2020, https://twitter.com/rgay/status/1220034745246998528.

5. Anthroplogie, "Our Promise to Our Community," July 8, 2020, https://www.anthropologie.com/en-gb/diversity-and-inclusion.

6. Toni Morrison, *Beloved* (New York: Knopf, 1987).

7. Republicworld.com, "Colin Kaepernick Net Worth, Kneeling Protests and Reason Behind the End of His NFL Career," June 4, 2020, https://www.republicworld.com/sports-news/other-sports/colin-kaepernick-net-worth-kneeling-protests-reason-behind-career-end.html.

8. "Corporate America Has Failed Black America," *New York Times*, June 6, 2020, https://www.nytimes.com/2020/06/06/business/corporate-america-has-failed-black-america.html.

9. Color of Change, https://colorofchange.org, accessed December 2, 2020.

CHAPTER 8: LEADING BY EMPOWERING LISTENING

1. Imani Perry, @imaniperry, Twitter, June 11, 2020, 12:42 p.m., https://twitter.com/imaniperry/status/1271120554649681924.

2. S. Pinder-Amaker and C. Bell, "A Bioecological Approach for Addressing the College Mental Health Crisis," *Harvard Review of Psychiatry* 20, no. 4 (2012): 174–88.

3. Deloitte, "Waiter, Is That Inclusion in My Soup? A New Recipe to Improve Business Performance," research report, May 2013, https://www2.deloitte.com/content/dam/Deloitte/au/Documents/human-capital/deloitte-au-hc-diversity-inclusion-soup-0513.pdf.

CHAPTER 9: STAYING SAFE

1. *Get Out* was a widely acclaimed 2017 horror film written and directed by Jordan Peele. Peele wanted the audience watching the film to feel the anxiety of what it is like to be Black in America. The audience is introduced to Black characters who seem complicit with their subjection to dominant white characters, but are actually being mind-controlled.

CHAPTER 10: RESPONDING TO IDENTITY-RELATED AGGRESSIONS (IRAS)

1. M. Scully and M. Rowe, "Bystander Training Within Organizations," *Journal of the International Ombudsman Association* 2, no. 1 (2009): 1–9.

2. D. W. Sue et al., "Disarming Racial Microaggressions: Microintervention Strategies for Targets, White Allies, and Bystanders," *American Psychologist* 74, no. 1 (2019): 128–42.

3. Gina Torino, "How Racism and Microaggressions Lead to Worse Health," Centre for Health Journalism, November 10, 2017, https://center forhealthjournalism.org/2017/11/08/how-racism-and-microaggressions -lead-worse-health.

CHAPTER 13: ANTI-RACISM IN THE WORKPLACE

1. "Being Antiracist," National Museum of African American History and Culture, https://nmaahc.si.edu/learn/talking-about-race/topics/being -antiracist, accessed October 26, 2020.

2. Winters, *Black Fatigue*.

3. S. K. Kang et al., "Whitened Résumés: Race and Self-Presentation in the Labor Market," *Administrative Science Quarterly* 61, no. 3 (2016): 469–502, https://doi.org/10.1177/0001839216639577.

4. A. M. Carton and A. S. Rosette, "Explaining Bias Against Black Leaders: Integrating Theory on Information Processing and Goal-Based Stereotyping," *Academy of Management Journal* 54, no. 6 (2011): 1141–58.

5. Tsedale M. Melaku, "Why Women and People of Color in Law Still Hear 'You Don't Look Like a Lawyer,'" *Harvard Business Review*, August 7, 2019, https://hbr.org/2019/08/why-women-and-people-of-color-in-law-still -hear-you-dont-look-like-a-lawyer.

6. Mitu Gulati and Devon W. Carbado, "Race to the Top of the Corporate Ladder: What Minorities Do When They Get There," *Washington & Lee Law Review* 61 (2004): 1645–93.

7. G. M. Walton et al., "Stereotype Threat in Organizations: Implications for Equity and Performance," *Annual Review of Organizational Psychology and Organizational Behavior* 2 (2015): 523–50, https://doi.org/10.1146 /annurev-orgpsych-032414-111322.

8. P. F. Hewlin, "Wearing the Cloak: Antecedents and Consequences of Creating Facades of Conformity," *Journal of Applied Psychology* 94, no. 3 (2009): 727–41, doi:10.1037/a0015228.

9. Laura Morgan Roberts, Anthony J. Mayo, and David A. Thomas, eds., *Race, Work, and Leadership: New Perspectives on the Black Experience* (Boston: Harvard Business Review Press, 2019).

10. Robin DiAngelo, *White Fragility: Why It's So Hard for White People to Talk About Racism* (Boston: Beacon Press, 2018).

11. David A. Thomas and John J. Gabarro, *Breaking Through: The Making of Minority Executives in Corporate America* (Boston: Harvard Business School Press, 1999).

12. Roberts, Mayo, and Thomas, *Race, Work, and Leadership*.

13. Susanne Bruckmüller and Nyla R. Branscombe, "How Women End Up on the 'Glass Cliff,'" *Harvard Business Review*, January–February 2011.

14. M. K. Ryan et al., "'Think Crisis-Think Female: The Glass Cliff and Contextual Variation in the Think Manager-Think Male Stereotype," *Journal of Applied Psychology* 96, no. 3 (May 2011): 470–84.

15. Jaclyn Trop, "Is Mary Barra Standing on a 'Glass Cliff'?," *New Yorker*, April 29, 2014, https://www.newyorker.com/business/currency/is-mary-barra-standing-on-a-glass-cliff.

16. We don't presume that any space is truly "safe" when it comes to identities. Discussing identities within any relationship brings risk of invalidation or lack of support, even within a shared identity.

17. Victor Ray, "Why So Many Organizations Stay White," *Harvard Business Review*, November 19, 2019, https://hbr.org/2019/11/why-so-many-organizations-stay-white.

CHAPTER 14: FOLLOW THE DATA TO THE FUTURE

1. W. Carlezon Jr., "NPP Statement on Racism, Discrimination, and Abuse of Power," *Neuropsychopharmacology* 45 (2020): 1589–90, https://doi.org/10.1038/s41386-020-0739-3.

2. L. P. Wadsworth et al., "Ways to Boost Your Research Rigor Through Increasing Your Cultural Competence" (part 1 of 2), *Behavior Therapist* 39, no. 3 (2016): 76–82, 90–92.

# READING
# GUIDE

1. In chapter 1, "Inclusive Teams Are Better Teams," the authors outline the pitfalls of creating "diverse" workspaces without providing the necessary tools to support those of rising underrepresented identities who have been invited into the work environment. Beyond those outlined in the book, what are some ways in which you, on the individual level, might foster a safer environment in order to maintain a diverse team?

2. Are there times when you've witnessed either successes or failures of organizational diversity initiatives? What factors led to these successes and/or failures?

3. The authors coin the term IRAs (identity-related aggressions) to remove "micro" from the term "microaggressions." How does this shift in terminology change your perspective on IRAs? Can you think of any other commonly used terms in the context of identity and organizational reflection that might benefit from revision?

4. The authors assert that "One of the most insidious aspects of identity-related aggressions is that they occur without notice" (p. 21). How and where does this ring true in your experience? Reflect on thoughtful ways to draw attention to IRAs as they occur.

5. In a scenario involving Barnes & Noble's mishandling of publications related to Black History Month, the authors encourage the company to "re-approach," which means "making an informed

and sustained attempt to address the issue it originally sought to highlight" (p. 72). What factors make re-approaching a difficult process both for companies and for individuals? Have you ever had to redress an issue like that in this scenario? If so, reflect on the challenges, significance, and end results of this process.

6. The authors assert that a crucial first step in organizational assessment is for a system to acknowledge its history. What makes this action essential and how might you practice it in your own organization?

7. The authors coin the term "the action/savior fix" to define a moment wherein one takes ownership away from the target of a harmful situation by shifting the focus away from their pain and to your new mission (p. 93). How do intent and impact play a role in this "fix"? Have you ever been on the receiving end of the action/savior fix? If so, what role do you wish the "savior" would have taken in that moment, and what actionable steps can you think of that might guide them toward that role?

8. Think of a time wherein you either acted as or required an ally in a challenging situation. What characteristics do you value in an effective upstander? Why is it sometimes difficult to speak out as an upstander, and how might you overcome these difficulties?

9. *Did That Just Happen?!* goes into detail about fear surrounding the word "racist" and about the cultural hesitancy to name racist actions as they occur. Do you find it difficult to use this terminology? If so, what historical, social, or environmental factors contribute to your fears surrounding the word "racist"?

10. The authors note that the theme of safety recurs throughout this book "because cultural shifts cannot occur unless people feel safe to take risks" (p. 131). Envision a "safer space." What obstacles lie between your current work environment and the safer environment you've envisioned? What contributes or detracts from your sense of safety in the workplace?

11. The authors provide examples of what they term "the empowering apology" (p. 122). They note that "That was inappropriate and hurtful. I'm very sorry" or "I realize that my

12. assumption was racist. I'm very sorry" are two of many valid responses. Brainstorm your own empowering apologies. What are the most meaningful components of an empowering apology, and how did you incorporate these components into your own examples?

13. Identify the large cultural shifts you'd like to see take place in your organization. Why haven't these shifts yet occurred, and what can you do to actualize them?

# INDEX